Advance Praise for *Know Yourself, Grow Your* (

If you want a career that is both personally meaningful and financially viable, you will work hard, defer gratification, and accept a certain number of tradeoffs. But that's not enough. You will also need the courage to look within to understand who you really are, and you will need the honesty to examine what the world around you actually needs. These are complex questions that are not easily answered, which explains in part why so few people are willing to go there. But if you are among the willing, Anne Marie Segal's new book will be an invaluable resource to you on your journey. Her supportive but no-nonsense voice will guide you through the specific steps of figuring out who you are, identifying what value you bring to the world, and sharing all this in a way that will get you actual jobs. Be forewarned: this is a WORK book filled with tasks to do, not a set of career bromides to ponder. So roll up your sleeves, clear you head, and get started toward the life you actually want!

> – Michael F. Melcher, Author, *The Creative Lawyer* and host of the podcast, *Meanwhile*

To grow our careers and find satisfaction in our workdays, we all need to articulate the value we hold and benefits we bring to employers and clients. With *Know Yourself, Grow Your Career*, Anne Marie has simplified the conversation around creating a personal value proposition. Her workbook will help you create a self-driven vision for your professional life.

Know Yourself, Grow Your Career includes thoughtful, targeted questions to elicit your skills, talents, interests, values and preferences. And Anne Marie explains how to employ your strengths and professional priorities to create your own career path, which may include a role that does not exist yet.

If you want to accelerate your next move (whether it's up or off the ladder), use this book! Your career will thank you.

> – J. Kelly Hoey, Author, *Build Your Dream Network*

Know Yourself is a one-stop resource for anyone wanting to take charge of their career trajectory and do so from a place of integrity, authenticity and inner power. It guides the reader through every stage of the process with exactly the right questions and helpful examples. There are no false shortcuts here, but if you're willing to put in the work, you will emerge with a clear roadmap to the best version of your professional life.

> – Hyeon-Ju Rho, Leadership and Transition Coach

If you apply for jobs that are of no interest to you and then wonder why you aren't hired, you'd do well to stop the treadmill and break out this workbook. Believe me, the hiring manager can tell that you're a "cut and paste" expert but not actually applying to the job offered. Anne Marie's experience, know-how, and drive to help you succeed come through on each page.

> – Lucie Sandel, Associate Director of Professional Development, The University of Chicago

Know Yourself, Grow Your Career is equal parts practical "how-to" resource and inspirational read. Whether you are looking for a new job opportunity or seeking ways to better connect with the one that you currently have (or both), this book will help you get there. It is a road map for knowing, growing and sharing your worth that both illuminates a clear path and motivates you to begin traveling down it.

> – Jeff Marootian, Former Assistant Secretary,
>   U.S. Department of Transportation

As a career branding expert to executives, attorneys, and senior business leaders, I believe strongly in the power of creating a unique value proposition to help communicate a strong personal brand for job searches and leadership roles in today's digital age.

Through *Know Yourself*, Anne Marie has formulated a personalized workbook that enables professionals to extract their inner talent to grow their career effectively. This book, which also includes Anne Marie's leadership coaching value, will help professionals soar to new and exciting heights.

> – Wendi M. Weiner, Esq., Attorney, Writer, Career Branding Expert and
>   President-Elect of the National Resume Writers Association

If you're ready to level up your income and career, this book is your golden ticket.

Understanding, articulating and owning your value is critical to earning what you're worth. But it can be an intimidating trek and most people aren't sure where to begin. Or lack the objectivity to guide themselves through the process.

In *Know Yourself, Grow Your Career*, Anne Marie has done the heavy lifting by asking all the essential questions. Your answers to those questions equip you with the ability to confidently ask for — and get — the position and pay you want.

If you're truly motivated to create a more rewarding future, this book is the map you need for your journey.

> – Carolyn Herfurth, Activator. Accelerator. Adventurer.

Anne Marie Segal does the nearly impossible with *Know Yourself, Grow Your Career*. With masterful precision yet flexibility to enable each individual job seeker to deeply self-examine, she first draws job seekers through the soul search essential to developing a meaningful personal value proposition. Then, she helps them focus sometimes ethereal ideas into real-world terms, giving job seekers both the strategy and the technique to sell themselves professionally. I look forward to recommending this highly practical workbook to my clients.

> – Amy L. Adler, MBA, Certified Master Resume Writer

Know Yourself is an essential guidebook for anyone looking to transition in their careers but questioning where to turn or looking to leverage their current career trajectory. It is a unique mixture of reflective journaling and concrete action steps that leave the reader feeling confident and in command of their journey ahead.

Many of us may want to take that next step in our career but hold back because of fear, our nagging inner critique and ambiguity about where and how to start. This book is your answer to all those objections.

> — Cathy Sorbara, COO of Cheeky Scientist and one of 70 women
> scientists participating in the groundbreaking Homeward Bound
> journey to Antarctica in 2018

Know Yourself, Grow Your Career addresses the all too often forgotten element of the value proposition in a candidate's career search. Understanding where we are in our careers and what we want next, and articulating those skills, strengths and experiences so we are well understood and thereby positioned to make the next great move in our careers, cannot be emphasized enough.

I have often called the value proposition the spine of a career campaign. Anne Marie Segal helps the individual job seeker turn this daunting task into manageable steps, resulting in a most satisfactory career!

> — Linda M. Van Valkenburgh, Owner & Executive Coach,
> My Executive Career Coach, LLC

Our work lives occupy the lion's share of our waking hours, whether you are an executive or someone just starting out. Success and personal satisfaction in your work life substantially enriches your professional journey. There are many factors that lead to professional success – hard work, the willingness to collaborate, maintaining a learning mindset – are just a few.

Yet just as important, if not more so, is self-knowledge and self-awareness. Understanding ourselves and who we are has a powerful impact on how we approach the challenges and responsibilities that confront us and will be invaluable as we embrace or face work life transitions. With Anne Marie Segal's newest book, *Know Yourself, Grow Your Career*, she walks the reader through the process of a self-assessment and reflection that is thoughtful, objective and designed to help each individual honestly build and better understand their personal value proposition.

The book is a wonderful tool for those taking on the challenge of identifying and embracing the right path to greater professional success and satisfaction.

> — Catherine L. Reed, National Development Professional

Generosity lives at the core of this comprehensive guide. Anne Marie has shaped personal value proposition creation into a deeply meaningful process.

I will definitely keep this results-oriented resource within arms reach and recommend it to my clients!

> – Elena Deutsch, Leadership & Career Coach,
> Creator of WILL, Women Interested in Leaving (big) Law

In Anne Marie Segal's first book, *Master the Interview*, she gave great advice on how to nail the interview. However, before you even get to the interview, you should know your value proposition.

Know Yourself, Grow Your Career: The Personal Value Proposition Workbook should be the first thing anyone does before revising or sending out their resume. You need to know where you want to go with your career in order to get there. If you don't control your career path, before long your career path will control you.

As a legal recruiter, I have seen too many candidates get stuck in niches that hold no interest for them. Once you are typecast in a practice area, it is very hard to change, so the earlier you learn what works for you, the better. If every law student had to go through Anne Marie's book, *Know Yourself*, I believe there would be happier attorneys with less turnover.

Yet many people spend more time planning a family vacation than planning their career. Don't be fooled: the *Know Yourself* workbook is hard work. You will need to spend the time to create a road map for your career. Remember, even if you do this right out of law school - or college, for that matter - there will be plenty of opportunities to take a different path. You will want to keep your exercises and journal handy to continue the journey to retirement.

Once you know your path, work with a recruiter that hears your needs and desires. Many positions are not listed on the internet. A good recruiter will identify the right position and law firm or company culture to fit your career goals.

Take this time to plan your career. Don't let time slip away. Get started immediately!

> – Shari Davidson, Legal Recruiter and President,
> On Balance Search Consultants LLC

KNOW YOURSELF, GROW YOUR CAREER:

THE PERSONAL VALUE PROPOSITION WORKBOOK

ANNE MARIE SEGAL

*****

Cover Image:

Author Photograph:

ISBN 978-0-692-94087-7

Publications may be available at special discounts when purchased in bulk for fundraising, educational or organizational use. Book excerpts or summaries may also be created to specification for proprietary workshop or other uses. Please direct any inquiries with details about the query to knowyourself@segalcoaching.com.

In memory of my grandparents, for their laughter and love –

Jack, Ruth, Ralph and Margaret

ACKNOWLEDGEMENTS

I would like to thank my clients, colleagues, close and extended friends, family and others for their constant stream of questions and ideas, including those professionals and students who have attended my presentations.

In particular, I thank Lada Šoljan, Lucie Sandel, Jean Austin, Victoria Zerjav, Sally Cordovano, Isaiah Hankel, Diane Safer, Bridget Fox, Lee Cushman, Matthew Garnett, Dan Hoeyer, Colleen Mulligan, Maribel Rivera and others who have invited me to speak to their organizations about developing a personal value proposition and related topics.

I would also like express my heartfelt gratitude to a special group of seven peer advisors who read early copies and iterations of this book and graced me with their personal feedback: Kristen DeMarco, Stacey Schwartz, Karin Wolfe, Robyn Davis, Judy Siegel, Elizabeth Urdang and Lada Šoljan. I am extremely appreciative of their insights, constructive criticism and questions throughout the process of writing this book. Each of these early readers, in the course of multiple drafts, conversations and emails, made a unique contribution to the depth and character of this book.

Further appreciation goes to Susan Whitcomb, founder of The Academies (at which I completed my career management coach training), for providing the seeds that grew into a number of the ideas that appear in this book; Donna Sweidan, founder of Careerfolk, LLC, for introducing me to career coaching and letting me "shadow" her as I gained experience; and Kim Avery, for teaching me how to open up to the experience of being a coach.

Lastly, many others have given me pivotal advice, recognition or support at key points in my career. I wanted to include them all, but I found myself with a list of almost 100 names. I will shorten it to nine former professors and work colleagues of mine who have made a lasting, positive impact and truly shaped the course of my career: Reinhold Heller, John Sexton, Martha Schneider, Catherine Edelman, David Robbins, Larry Gannon, Margery Colloff, Arthur Amron and Gloria Skigen. The first two were my master's thesis advisor at The University of Chicago and the former Dean of NYU Law School (who was also my 1-L Civil Procedure professor, for those who can appreciate all that entails), respectively.

As I have expressed before and surely will again, I am also blessed to have a husband, children and extended family members who believe in me and made time for this project in our busy schedules. I am forever grateful to them.

My daughter still wants me to write a novel, and I agree – *I will!*

TABLE OF CONTENTS

Foreword 13

Introduction 14

Schedule 17

Action Items 18

PART 1: YOUR PRIORITIES AND STRENGTHS

Unit 1: The Roadmap 20

Unit 2: Self-Reflection 24

Unit 3: Clarity 43

Unit 4: Skills 55

Unit 5: Talents 75

PART 2: MARKET NEEDS

Unit 6: Understanding Market Needs 84

PART 3: CREATING A MATCH

Unit 7: Your Value Proposition 100

Unit 8: Creating Your Own Market 119

PART 4: COMMUNICATING YOUR VALUE

Unit 9: Your Personal Brand 130

Unit 10: Your Elevator Pitch(es) 140

Conclusion 154

Final Notes
About the Author

FOREWORD

Are you ready to make a greater impact in your career and feel more satisfied with the working hours of your day?

This book will help you do the invaluable work of getting to know yourself better and articulating your value so that you can grow your professional life in a way that appropriately challenges and inspires you, provides tangible and intangible rewards and – if it's one of your professional values – serves a greater good. To do that, you need to start with a creative and open mindset, trust that these goals are possible and dedicate yourself to achieve them.

For professionals who are driven by practical results or service to other people or causes, investing in measured, reflective time on one's own needs can seem unproductive, self-indulgent or both. We feel it is a luxury we cannot afford, a waste of time. I assure you it is not. As we all know, we have to put on our own oxygen masks first, then assist others.

As you start working through this book, you will see that Unit 2 (the first set of workbook exercises) is devoted to reconnecting with your interests and values, some of which are directly on point with your professional life and others that (for some of us, at least) are more personal. This is highly intentional. Many of us lost touch with what matters to us most, caught up in the drama of everyday life. A deep dive into our interests and values helps us reawaken our creative sides and create a self-driven vision for our professional lives.

What is creativity? Merriam-Webster's dictionary refers to creativity as the "ability to make new things or think of new ideas." Creativity is also about being open to and making new connections, seeing common things in a novel way, experimenting, inventing and living in a state of curiosity. There are at least a thousand more ways to see or "define" creativity, and you can take your inspiration from anywhere, anything or anyone, including Albert Einstein, Maya Angelou, Simon Sinek or Dr. Seuss.

> If one is lucky, a solitary fantasy can totally transform one million realities.
> - *Maya Angelou*

If you can get in touch with your creativity, the following pages will be an adventure, not a chore. This is *your* workbook. Use it in a way that brings fulfillment and results for *you*.

INTRODUCTION

How to Use this Book

This book is divided into ten units and can be used as a guide for individual coaching, workshops or your own exploration. If you are working with Segal Coaching, please visit www.annemariesegal.com/pvpcoaching and enter the password provided.

What is a Personal Value Proposition?

If we start with the Oxford dictionary definition of value proposition, a marketing concept, we see that it means "innovations or services intended to make a company, organization, service or product attractive to customers."

So how does this translate for people?

We all, in our jobs, businesses or other contributions to the world, need to understand how we can *convert what we offer into something others need*. In a nutshell, what we offer to others is our personal value proposition.

Throughout this book I call the "others" in the above paragraph the "market," as most of us need and want to monetize what we offer (i.e., be compensated for our work). Defining a personal value proposition helps us do that more effectively with more satisfying results, including better compensation levels for work that we enjoy.

You often cannot discern your personal value proposition in a single step or through a logical, even algorithmic function (although some computer programs purport to do just that). There are several reasons why a more individualized approach is needed. First, unlike products or services like groceries or transportation, your value proposition is very complex, encompassing a range of factors you may not yet have learned to vocalize and impacted by your interests, values, personality, talents and skills. Only by knowing yourself and internalizing that knowledge can you find the best match of your strength to market needs.

Second, growing disruptions in the marketplace have affected public perception and delivery of services. For example, what is a "phone" or "phone service" nowadays? It's not as simple as it was 20 years ago. In the wireless space, for example, it is taken for granted that "phone service" includes instant messaging, texting and other communication capabilities beyond bilateral conversation. In the same way, the value we can add to employers or clients is not as straightforward as it once was. Indeed, prospective clients and employers often appreciate or expect people they hire to possess value beyond their substantive skill set. Imagine a young lawyer who is hired not only for her legal knowledge and trial experience but also for proficiencies far afield from the traditional lawyering subset, such as social media skills.

If we go back to the value proposition concept above and apply it to ourselves, **what innovations and services do we most want to offer and to what extent will the market compensate us for them? What considerations and tradeoffs should we consider as**

part of our analysis? Whether you are reading this book for career transition, advancement or business development, these are the points we seek to define here.

The Concepts Behind this Book

For many months after publishing my first book, *Master the Interview: A Guide for Working Professionals*, I led seminars and worked with clients on an individual basis to help professionals and students develop their personal value propositions.

It struck me how many of them found the concept of a personal value proposition extremely challenging to define, even marketing professionals who were accustomed to thinking of value proposition as applied to abstract and concrete products and services. In the busy modern world, it seems, we have lost awareness of ourselves and become wrapped up in our careers without sufficient reflection of why we are in them.

At the same time, I often heard concerns about whether people could find jobs that were "interesting" or would be paid what they were "worth," without an accompanying exploration and identification of what interesting even meant or the unique value they might offer in exchange for the compensation sought. As a coach, I help clients reframe these questions in a way that is more productive:

~~Will they make it interesting for me?~~

~~Will they pay me what I am worth?~~

Reframe as:

How can I take on challenges that are interesting to me?

What value can I add to increase my worth?

To reap the benefits of reframing, it may be necessary to change jobs. There are some jobs that cannot be remade to fit one's interests or (newly-discovered) value proposition, no matter how much we may try. At other times, a fresh outlook can change everything.

When I have presented these concepts to scores of professionals - many of whom are mid-level or senior executives - I have discovered that many of us need some quality time getting more familiar with ourselves to flesh out each of the elements of the formula. **In fact, the more hard-driving and successful we are, the more we may benefit from reflecting on our personal value propositions – independent of job requirements for our current roles – as what worked to get us where we are may no longer be working.** This discovery prompted the workbook you have in your hands.

At times, we overestimate our ability to match what we seek to the needs of the market and what it is (i.e., people and companies) are poised to pay us to do. More often, we underestimate our ability to match our unique sets of needs and strengths to the market and create opportunities where they do not appear, at first glance, to exist.

Do not expect to breeze through this workbook in a weekend. I might kindly suggest that if your time available and commitment level is so limited, you will be better served with another resource. (See, for example, the abridged personal value proposition worksheets on my website.) While you can work at your own pace and complete as much or as little as you need here, to be effective this process does require some time commitment. The exercises in this book are designed to help you create that elusive balance and gain needed clarity to reframe and grow your career (and, if you embrace it, your personal life). Enjoy the journey as you discover and learn to leverage your value proposition.

One last point on the exercises: Since we all see read words on the page differently, if an exercise is unclear to you or seems to merit multiple answers, interpret it in the way that yields the best results for your self-discovery. This is a starting point to help generate ideas, not a quiz to be passed.

ANNE MARIE SEGAL
Founder and Executive Coach
Segal Coaching

You can reach and find me online as follows:

For coaching: asegal@segalcoaching.com

About the book: knowyourself@segalcoaching.com

Website and blog: www.annemariesegal.com

SCHEDULE

Whether you are completing this workbook on your own or as part of a coaching workshop or other group program, it is helpful to set and keep a schedule for completion.

Today's Date   _____, 20__

Target Completion Date   _____, 20__

With the above in mind – which you can reset if needed – you can record the actual completion dates of each unit so you can gauge your progress against your targets. While there is no race to finish and life may hand you other priorities – give yourself a realistic amount of time, based on your goals – a bit of healthy internal competition may propel you forward on the days (and there will be some) that staying the course is a struggle.

If you are working through this book over an extended period of time, you can offer yourself support in the form of organized goals, either in advance or unit by unit.

	Interim Target Date	Completion Date
Unit 1	_____, 20__	_____, 20__
Unit 2	_____, 20__	_____, 20__
Unit 3	_____, 20__	_____, 20__
Unit 4	_____, 20__	_____, 20__
Unit 5	_____, 20__	_____, 20__
Unit 6	_____, 20__	_____, 20__
Unit 7	_____, 20__	_____, 20__
Unit 8	_____, 20__	_____, 20__
Unit 9	_____, 20__	_____, 20__
Unit 10 (finally!)	_____, 20__	_____, 20__

ACTION ITEMS

Record for easy access any major "a-ha" moments that generate action items while working through this book:

_____

_____

_____

_____

_____

_____

_____

_____

_____

_____

_____

_____

_____

_____

_____

_____

_____

_____

PART 1:

YOUR PRIORITIES AND STRENGTHS

UNIT 1 - THE ROADMAP

For many of us, the need (or desire) to work will accompany most of our adult lives, and a personal value proposition facilitates our careers in a number of key ways.

First, a personal value proposition arms us with a better understanding of the type of roles for which we are best suited, feel engaged and can make meaningful contributions.

At the same time, we all undervalue ourselves. By defining a personal value proposition, we are able to affirmatively state our worth and build our confidence from the inside out.

Third, a clear personal value proposition is the basis for "personal branding" and elevator pitches – that we are often urged to define and have at the ready – in each case to properly position ourselves in front of connections, clients, peers, firm leadership, hiring managers, recruiters and others. An elevator pitch or personal brand based on anything less leads to a shallow, hollow reflection that requires too much energy to maintain and does not actually lead us in the direction that we seek (or would seek, with such self-knowledge at hand).

To illustrate this pyramid of personal value proposition, branding and elevator pitches, I have often used the following or a similar set of images:

One or more elevator pitches

short, distinct and persuasive summaries of your personal value proposition, which can and should be tailored to your audience

Personal branding

the impression you create (actively, in line with your personal value proposition, or passively) when interacting with others, including your topics of conversation, word choice, tone, outlook, attire, etc.

To create a consistent result, have a consistent brand.

Personal value proposition

the people you serve, problems you solve and benefits you bring
(with examples that support the story you have to tell)

An authentic personal value proposition, at the base of the pyramid, supports both your elevator pitches and personal branding (covered in Part 4 of this book), helping you build credibility among your audience.

Your PVP Equation

After various iterations of the component parts that, collectively, comprise one's personal value proposition, I have boiled it down to the following equation:

Your Priorities + Your Strengths + Market Needs =

Your Personal Value Proposition

An ideal career fits your needs while allowing you to use and grow your strengths.

YOUR PRIORITIES

YOUR PRIORITIES are what makes a role a good fit for you personally (and, by extension, make you a good fit for the job) because they express where you are motivated to invest your greatest time and efforts. Priorities can be broken down into interests, values and preferences.

Interests are what you enjoy, prefer and/or are personally committed to do, **values** are how you find and generate meaning and **preferences** reflect your work style, character and temperament.

YOUR STRENGTHS

YOUR STRENGTHS (which you also may have heard described as "competencies") can be further broken down into your skills and talents.

Skills are concrete, substantive areas of proficiency that you hold, have achieved or can achieve through focused efforts. **Talents** are what come naturally or easily to you, whether innately or through repeated exposure.

MARKET NEEDS

MARKET NEEDS, on the other hand, are roles that exist currently or could exist in the future if sufficient demand is created. Broad and niche markets for your strengths can include traditional employers as well as a larger audience (e.g., clients, consulting engagements, investors or donors).

As an specific example, public speaking may be part of your value proposition if you enjoy speaking to groups (**interests and preferences**) and/or are committed to a cause or organization that you want to advance through public speaking (**values**), invest the time to become a leader comfortable speaking to groups (**skill**) or have an affinity for it (**talent**) and accurately perceive a demand for your services on the proposed topics (**market needs**).

Your Priorities

Interests

Values

Preferences

Market Needs

Roles that exist currently or could exist in the future if demand is created

Your Strengths

Skills

Talents

**Your
Personal Value Proposition**

The match of your priorities and strengths with market needs, which includes:

- the people you serve,

- the problems you solve, and

- the benefits you bring

Here is how these might play out for a mid-level marketing professional (let's call him Alex):

Alex's interests are to continue to inject his quirky storytelling style and design into marketing campaigns, work more directly with clients, move into a management role and, if possible, travel internationally. He also would be keen to incorporate his love of nature and animals into his work product or workday, as long as it does not limit his options.

Alex's values include his desire to creating marketing materials that make a difference in people's lives, not just sell products. He also is committed to working on behalf of children on the autism spectrum (such as his nephew), especially finding ways to increase their employment opportunities, which he already does in his spare time.

One of **Alex's preferences** is to work autonomously, but he also likes how a team provides the ability to bounce ideas off each other. He likes quiet work environments in which people are serious about their work, and he cannot stand people who take credit for others' ideas.

Alex's skills include marketing strategy, social media, relationship-building, research, writing, design and other areas, in addition to fluency in Spanish and proficiency in Chinese. He is a master of project management and meeting deadlines, even on tight time frames.

Alex's talents include an uncanny ability to translate the pulse of current events to marketing campaigns, although he is still growing his awareness of how to craft these messages without offending anyone. He has strong leadership capacity and is well liked, but he has not held any recent leadership roles (his last one being Eagle Scout in high school).

As Alex investigates **market needs**, he will need to consider the strengths above as well as others he may uncover. First, Alex can evaluate *his current firm*. Is his quirky marketing style an asset to their client base? Does the firm value his strengths? Will they develop his talents and promote him? Is the environment conducive to doing his best work?

Alex can also seek out *other marketing agencies* that are looking for employees they can groom into leaders/partners as well as those in need of his specific skills and talents. He must be careful to temper his priorities with deep consideration of which roles will best suit and support his strengths, but he should not discount his priorities either, as they can help ensure a better long-term fit and may even give him an edge in some companies.

If Alex has the resources, temperament and desire to start *his own firm*, he may consider what additional skills will be needed for launch, growth and beyond on a daily, quarterly and annual basis. Most importantly, he will need to grow his skill for relationship-building into a new skill for client-generation. He may incorporate his interest in travel into his value proposition, offering it as an asset to clients who seek a smaller firm to service a larger area, including those focused on social media campaigns. Alex may have more autonomy at his own firm and a greater ability to craft his own message, but he should be aware of his desire to interact with a team (by building his own or through collaboration with others).

UNIT 2 - SELF-REFLECTION

Ask young children what they enjoy, and there is no end to the telling. Bike riding, baseball, piano, Play-doh®, computers, cartwheels, storytelling, soccer…. The list goes on.

As children start to grow up, preferences further evolve. For example, some love being with friends every minute of the day, while others are more drawn to spending lots of time on their own, in a world of their own creation.

As adults, many of us have lost touch with our evolving interests. Or rather, our interests have stopped evolving and are receding instead. We blame this on less time available to us – which is true – but must also admit we often are very narrowly focused and specialized in our day jobs and have lost a sense of wonder about our professional and personal interests. This state of being is so common that I am no longer surprised when I ask coaching clients, "what are your interests?" and hear back, "I don't actually know…."

Your priorities determine your fit with the culture and values of an organization, an individual team or clients. Clarifying your own needs helps you create an authentic value proposition that truly adds value for you as well as others, as you are putting your best self forward, leading to better job performance, relationships and health.

If you are one of those fortunate souls who is highly in touch with your interests, values and preferences, this unit should be a piece of (your favorite) cake. If you are not (or wish you were more of) that person, complete as much as you need to help you light that spark again.

> Note: If you are not in an emotional space at the moment that allows quiet contemplation of your own interests and needs, you may start with **Sections A, E and J** and later return to other exercises that will help develop your career vision. You may also wish to flip to **Section C of Unit 3**.

A. OVERVIEW OF MY PROFESSIONAL LIFE

How I found (or created) my current professional role:

Top activities that consume my days (as part of my job, volunteer work or self-direction):

What I love most about my work:

What I never want to do again (and would delegate if I could do so effectively):

On a scale of 1 to 10, I am a "people person" (1 = not really and 10 = very much):

1   2   3   4   5   6   7   8   9   10

What I like most about working with people:

What people like most about working with me:

How much of my day is spent working with people:

On a scale of 1 to 10, I am a "problem solver" (1 = not really and 10 = very much):

1   2   3   4   5   6   7   8   9   10

What problems I like to solve (list by theme, substance or otherwise):

What problems I am best at solving:

How much of my day is spent problem solving:

My work personality tends more toward: ___ introspection/thinking, ___ action/doing or ___ both. Notes and caveats: _____

Some benefits I derive from this personality:

Some opportunities I miss:

I am more comfortable when I have ___ options or ___ closure.

Generally, I ___ have or ___ don't have the options or closure I seek in my current role.

I expect a great return on my time invested: ___ yes ___ not necessarily ___ sometimes

How I measure that return (rank or check all that apply):

___ financially ___ whom or how I have been able to help ___ personal satisfaction

___ other _____

My "return on time investment" approach comes ___ naturally or ___ from experience.

What motivates me to go to work in the morning:

What I do when I don't feel motivated:

B. OVERVIEW OF MY PERSONAL LIFE

How I spend most of my free time:

News I read first:

Types or titles of books I find engaging:

Places I am always (or often) visiting:

Websites I have bookmarked or visit often:

Special interests (from clocks to cybersecurity, fashion to fantasy football, health to house renovations, math to marathons, trees to transportation, or wine to wildlife):

How I connect with my interests (volunteering, board service, leisure activities, travel, etc.):

Inventions or ideas that I have created, wish I had brought to market or still may launch:

What I would make time for, if I only had the time (ironic, right?):

What always makes me laugh:

What always makes me cry:

What I would do if I did not need to earn a living:

If I could travel to five new (or returning) places, they would be:

If I could live anywhere in the world, it would be:

Foreign languages I speak (or wish I had learned):

Movies I love:

Sports I love:

Music I love (playing or listening to), including my top five favorite songs:

Favorite summer and winter activities:

Favorite foods (and any special food preferences, allergies, etc.) to cook and eat:

C. RECONNECTING WITH MY YOUNGER SELF

If I could go back to school, I would study:

What I learned about "work" from my parents and extended family:

What I loved to create when I was younger (write or draw it here):

What I felt passionate about earlier in my life:

My favorite places to hide as a child:

Times I felt safe as a child:

My childhood heroes:

D. HEALTH

I keep myself **physically** healthy by:

_____

_____

I keep myself **mentally** healthy by:

_____

_____

I keep myself **financially** healthy by:

_____

_____

I keep myself **spiritually** healthy by:

_____

_____

I keep myself **emotionally** healthy by:

_____

_____

E. MY VALUES

The values and/or principles I would fight for most are:

_____

_____

My identity would not feel complete if I lost:

_____

_____

My life needs more (e.g. peace, order, autonomy, quality time, rest, fame, achievement, etc.):

_____

_____

The world needs more (and I can contribute by):

_____

_____

My field or workplace needs more (and I can contribute by):

_____

_____

I could not live without (personally or professionally):

_____

_____

I feel most proud of:

_____

_____

I feel most passionate about:

_____

_____

I have as professional mentors:

_____

_____

Those I most admire personally or professionally are:

_____

_____

F. MEANING

THE MOST MEANINGFUL THINGS
I HAVE DONE OR EXPERIENCED LATELY, AND EVER...

How I Define "Meaningful":

The Most Meaningful Things I Have Done This Month:

The Most Meaningful Things I Have Done This Year:

The Most Meaningful Things I Have Done in My Life:

What I find very meaningful but have not yet done:

What fills me with wonder (about the world and beyond):

Two-Week "Meaningful Moments" Tracker for the Weeks of _____

1st Monday Meaningful	2nd Monday Meaningful
1st Tuesday Meaningful	2nd Tuesday Meaningful
1st Wednesday Meaningful	2nd Wednesday Meaningful
1st Thursday Meaningful	2nd Thursday Meaningful
1st Friday Meaningful	2nd Friday Meaningful
1st Saturday Meaningful	2nd Saturday Meaningful
1st Sunday Meaningful	2nd Sunday Meaningful

How conducting this experiment helped reframe my thoughts about what I find meaningful:

My best friends and closest family members are:

This is how I bond with them:

Here is what they add to my life:

Here are some types of people, places or things I don't like (and why):

If I could live at any time in history, it would be (and why):

G. COMFORT ZONE QUESTIONS

Personally, I feel most in my comfort zone when:

_____

_____

_____

Professionally, I feel most in my comfort zone when:

_____

_____

_____

I have succeeded in environments that:

_____

_____

_____

_____

I just can't stop doing (because I get in the "flow"):

_____

_____

_____

_____

Things or ideas that push me beyond my comfort zone (that I <u>enjoy</u>) include:

_____

_____

_____

Things or ideas that push me beyond my comfort zone (that <u>throw me off</u>) include:

_____

_____

_____

_____

What I do when that happens:

_____

_____

_____

_____

I would rather:

___ Live completely within my comfort zone

___ Be challenged from time to time

___ Be in the presence of others who continually challenge me

___ Other _____

_____

Things I obsess about – good or bad – that everyone knows:

_____

_____

_____

Things I obsess about – good or bad – that those close to me know:

_____

_____

_____

Things I obsess about – good or bad – that nobody knows:

_____

_____

_____

To me, failure is:

_____

_____

And success is:

_____

_____

If I could have multiple lives, some other things I would do personally or professionally (that I can't do now) would be:

_____

_____

_____

_____

If I consider the phrase, "I would do what I really wanted in life if 'X' were true," my X is:

_____

_____

_____

_____

Can X be changed? __ Yes __ No   How (or why not)? _____

_____

_____

H. MORE DEEP DIVING

If I had complete discretion on how to use my time, I would:

If I had a weekend next month to do whatever I wanted, I would:

If I could change anything about the world, it would be:

If I could speak on any topic (including past topics, if any), I would speak about:

If I wrote a book (or my next book, if I have written one already), I would write about:

If I started a charity or spearheaded a new cause, it would be in support of:

If I told people what I really thought about important parts of my life, they would be:

___ Excited   ___ Nervous   ___ Surprised   ___ Other _____

Five years from now, I will look back and wish I had changed this about my life today:

I. SUMMING UP

How I would rank my own self-awareness *before* this exercise:

1   2   3   4   5   6   7   8   9   10

How I rank it *after* this exercise:

1   2   3   4   5   6   7   8   9   10

Key priorities that have emerged from my answers:

_____

_____

_____

What surprised me the most:

_____

_____

_____

Questions that I want to explore further:

_____

_____

_____

_____

Ways I can keep myself open and the momentum going:

_____

_____

_____

_____

J. THEMES

Record any themes that have emerged from your answers above:

Interests:
Values:
Preferences:

K. TRANSFORMATION

If your immediate goals in working through this unit are not only to arrive at your personal value proposition but also increase your value, you may wish to complete this final section.

My interest in transforming or (re)launching my career or business (with 10 as the highest):

1   2   3   4   5   6   7   8   9   10

My commitment to transforming or (re)launching my career or business:

1   2   3   4   5   6   7   8   9   10

If my answers are on the high end, what I can do to make that happen:

Professional interests with which I would like to reconnect:

People with whom it would be helpful to connect who share these interests:

How and when I plan to connect with them:

What about my life would need to change to make room for these interests:

How I can expand my comfort zone to help me reconnect with these interests:

How I can further process and move beyond what is holding me back (my "X" on page 37):

Who in my life will need to be part of the change and how they can help:

How I can help them in return:

What else I would like to change and how I can do it:

UNIT 3 - CLARITY

Our exploration of our interests, values and preferences is an ever-evolving process. The more clarity we can gain, the more fluid and rewarding our professional lives will become.

This unit is divided into four parts. If you found some of the exercises in Unit 2 challenging or you want further guidance as you continue to meditate on your career needs, please work through one or more of the first three parts of this unit.

If you are ready to set your professional priorities, you can turn directly to **Section C** starting on **page 50**.

A. EMBRACING (AND TEMPERING?) YOUR NATURAL TENDENCIES

In the prior unit, I asked you to consider whether you lean more toward one or the other on the spectrum of thinking versus doing. Let's unpack the contrast:

The Introspective Crowd: who <u>observe</u> the world, take in information and enjoy introspection. They make careful, calculated decisions, without rushing to judgment.

The Results-Oriented Crowd: who charge ahead with a goal in mind, <u>ready to take on</u> the world. They are comfortable making decisions with limited information.

It is likely that neither approach completely sums you up – we humans are complex – but that you have strong tendencies one way or another. You may find that if you are a Results-Oriented person, you may need frequent vacations to relax and recharge. If you are one of the Introspective types, on the other hand, there may be urgent situations in your life in which you have increased adrenaline and channel your inner Point A-to-B mindset, and then you ease back into your "normal" self when the situation passes.

Some of us may naturally (i.e., without extra attention or effort) tend toward one or the other and wish that we could achieve more balance or flip our tendency to the other side. If you are in that situation, it can be helpful to ask yourself what you hope to achieve through the change. For example, you may have received feedback that you are always two steps ahead of your team and need to slow down and become more inclusive, or that your health is suffering because you are always in a state of stress. On the other hand, if you wish to move your career to the next level (management, senior management, owner, etc.) and want to become more goal-oriented, you may need to practice in-the-moment decision-making and accept the inevitable mistakes (and some failures, which are learning experiences) that may accompany it.

My initial thoughts about self-reflection versus action and whether I wish to embrace my natural tendencies, create more balance or "try on" how the world might look differently if my tendencies were reversed (see next page):

My Thoughts on Self-Reflection versus Action

The goal is not to be one type or another but instead to be aware of and comfortable with the entirety of your choice. You may have heard yourself saying, for example:

"I would love to move up, but I am just not interested in making the sacrifices it requires...."

or

"I feel very accomplished, so why I am not satisfied with what I have done?"

These may sound like two sides of the same coin, but if you read more closely the first phrase expresses an internal decision (being "not interested") and assumes external factors at play (that more sacrifices would be required, which is often true but could be further explored in more detail, before a final decision is made) and the second expresses an entirely internal dilemma (which may actually have external factors). In other words, behind either of these phrases, is there more going on?

This is where language – vocalizing or writing out what we *really* mean – becomes so important. If you have a nagging feeling about your career trajectory that you cannot name, keep digging until you get there. For example, since we have been discussing some personality factors above, have you felt that you missed opportunities because you did not push ahead, and are you comfortable with your choices? (You cannot change the past, but you can learn from it.) By contrast, if you have been pushing ahead for your entire career, is it now time to reconnect with other aspects of your life? How you answer these questions creates a framework for the important work you will be doing in these units.

These tendencies reflect our interests, values and preferences, and they may manifest themselves (as we will discuss further in later chapters) as talents and skills as well.

I foreshadow skills here because of the interplay between your skills and interests. Anything can become a skill, including what may otherwise seem like an inherent personality trait (such as curiosity), if we have sufficient *interest* in acquiring that skill. We can become more skilled at speeding up, and we can become more skilled at slowing down.

Return on Investment (ROI) Approach

As another example, most of us will never play professional basketball or tennis, but many of us can, if we are interested and have *minimal* talent, improve our skills to the level that we could join (or win) a weekly game on the court. This is where the question of return on investment (ROI) comes into place, which is a thrust of this unit. If you could acquire the skills to join or lead a group of local players on the court Thursday nights, and it would take you 100 hours in practice time and/or cost $500 in lessons to do that, you can then ask yourself, "what's my end game?" The more you are motivated to make something happen, the more you are willing to invest in it (and the more likely you are to achieve your goals).

An ROI-based approach to life puts you somewhere between the two personality types I mention above. You are neither exclusively charging ahead nor entirely taking an introspective, measured approach. Instead, you are asking **what efforts you reasonably believe must be expended to have a strong likelihood of achieving certain results** and whether that investment of effort is something you are willing to undertake, with an acceptance of the fact that **you only have control over your efforts, not the outcome**.

Again, the fact that there is uncertainty of any outcome is one of the reasons we are engaged in this self-analysis (Units 1-5). The one element in life that none of us can invent or buy more of is time. When we invest our time wisely – in ways that bring us closer to what we value in our lives – we improve our ability to predict outcomes.

But I Can't (and Similar Phrases)…

Small aside here: If you are afflicted by "I can't" or similar language, then you need all but to remove that phrase from your vocabulary. "I can't" should be reserved for situations in which you have a true restriction or derive a clear benefit from saying no. (For example, "I need to pass my exam next week, so I can't take on a new project today.")

As I said above, the language we choose is important because it helps us define what we really mean. What does your own **"I can't…"** phrase mean? Does it mean (as it often does) that if you make a certain choice, it could create discomfort in another aspect of your life?

A helpful approach is to ask what return you expect from an investment of your time, energy and funds, and whether the ROI is worth the effort to change. As every change has both positive and negative aspects, determining the ROI will help you motivate yourself to make changes that offer an appropriate level of risk and reward for your situation and goals.

"People-People" and "Problem Solvers"

Here's another personality trait question we explored in the last unit: are you more of a people-person or a problem-solver? Despite our collective emphasis on the importance of being a team player and the general human bias toward social interactions versus isolation, we are not all motivated primarily by social interactions 100% of the time. Many of us instead prefer tackling challenging problems rather than spending time in a room full of happy colleagues, and some might even endure an unpleasant work environment to do so.

Sometimes, over a period of time, the balance shifts. As I made the decision to change careers from law practice to coaching, for example, I had the opportunity to reflect on this shift for myself. I realized that while I was still drawn to intellectual challenges, I had become much more of a people-person during the latter span of my law career. I was no longer primarily driven by the challenge of sorting through and solving clients' complex legal issues (as I had been in the past); the personal, human connection took precedence.

Because my interests had shifted, my value proposition shifted as well. What I offered my employer and clients at the end of my legal career was entirely different from what I offered at the beginning, and it was not all attributable to moving from "newly-minted" to "experienced professional." Many of my prior colleagues, and people I know and respect in the legal and other professions, continue to be chiefly motivated by solving problems <u>for people</u> rather than maintaining a constant stream of personal interactions <u>with people</u>. I am now somewhere in the middle on this spectrum.

Where I am on the spectrum:

B. ACHIEVING FLOW

Staying on the results-driven track, let's revisit one of the questions in the last unit.

"Music I Love."

What did you write down in the prior unit about music you love? Now drill down deeper: *how do you connect with the songs you love?*

Here are some of the many ways in which we connect with songs:

Melody	Rhythm
Vocals	Instrumental
Message/Lyrics	Nostalgia/Memories
Mood	Energy

If you consistently connect with music, this exercise can help you understand more about yourself. Take a few minutes to recall your favorite songs and why you connect with them. Don't overthink it. This is mainly an emotional response, not a brain-driven exercise.

Song 1: _____

_____

Song 2: _____

_____

Song 3: _____

_____

Song 4: _____

_____

Song 5: _____

_____

What insights these connections give me:

_____

_____

_____

Getting in the Flow through Music and Other Favorite Activities

Did you notice that your mood improved as you "played" your favorite songs in your head? You may even be inspired to play or sing them aloud. Science tells us that music affects deep emotional centers in the brain, and as our emotions peak dopamine is released (as reported by diverse sources, from *Scientific American* to the BBC News).

Whether or not you can fathom the neuroscience, if I were to choose a single outcome for anyone reading this book, it would be that *this* state of flow and engagement is experienced during more hours of your day, with or without the music playing.

Music is not the only activity that helps us feel engaged, of course. Running can get us there, as can any other activity that stimulates us and awakens our emotions, so elect another activity if reflecting on your musical interests does not yield any fruitful results.

Ways my interests and values give me more energy and/or help me achieve flow:

What often breaks my flow and how I can address that:

On the next page, you can complete a two-week flow tracker. If at any point you find that you have become immersed in what you are doing – even losing track of time – write down what you were doing, the time of day and what initiated the flow.

Two-Week "When I Find Flow" Tracker for the Weeks of _____

1st Monday Flow	2nd Monday Flow
1st Tuesday Flow	2nd Tuesday Flow
1st Wednesday Flow	2nd Wednesday Flow
1st Thursday Flow	2nd Thursday Flow
1st Friday Flow	2nd Friday Flow
1st Saturday Flow	2nd Saturday Flow
1st Sunday Flow	2nd Sunday Flow

My observations about how I achieve this state and the role flow plays in my career:

It is likely obvious – although many of us tend to ignore or discount the fact – that we produce better work product if we are fully engaged with our work. If you develop a personal value proposition or take on roles that do not incorporate your interests in some way, it is easier to become burned out and lose focus and effectiveness.

Flow: Setting the Focus on Professional Activities

I intentionally did not give directions in the above exercise about whether your "flow tracking" should be on the personal or the professional front, but it is helpful now to shine some light specifically on the professional side. Thankfully, professional activities can be just as engaging as personal ones, if we seek out the right activities. Some people find their flow through advocacy or negotiations. Others like creating order out of chaos. Still others teach, write, invent or engage in other flow-producing activities. We should all learn what we find authentic and satisfying in our careers, beyond a paycheck.

Professional activities/challenges that bring me the greatest flow, enjoyment and rewards:

_____

_____

_____

_____

_____

Thoughts about the above:

_____

_____

_____

_____

Professional activities that drain my energy:

_____

_____

_____

_____

Areas of concern (if any) in my answers above:

_____

_____

_____

_____

How my flow analysis can help me connect with and strategize for my life and career:

_____

_____

_____

_____

_____

_____

C. SETTING PROFESSIONAL PRIORITIES

Until this point, we have discussed your personal and professional interests, values and preferences in an individual (rather than an organizational) context. For example, I asked what gets you fired up or, more literally, "what motivates you to go to work in the morning?" You may have given it some serious thought, or you may have simply written "coffee" or something else unrelated to professional goals, if you are utterly disenchanted with your role or company. (Not that I underestimate the power of coffee as a motivator!)

If you have more self-reflection to complete on an individual level, consider reviewing your prior answers or explore related questions that occurred to you. If you have a clear sense of yourself as an individual, it is time to assess how you function best as part of an organization.

It is crucial that we create sustainable value propositions that support our entire lives (work and home). At the same time, we need to understand our professional priorities and how we see ourselves contributing to an organizational structure.

Since we are in a unit addressing your priorities, consider not only your strengths but also your needs. Sometimes these answers may be prospective (e.g., if you are a new college graduate you will not be running the boardroom as your first career step, but if that is your goal, it is important to strategize about how you will get there). Answer what you believe is the best fit to reflect the contributions you wish to make in your career and, if appropriate, write in some early notes about what might need to happen to make these goals a reality (which we will cover further in later chapters).

If I could choose to be any member of the team within an organization, here is what I would most enjoy (check or circle all that apply and write any notes in the margins):

❑ Lead an organization as __ a board member and/or ___ senior management

❑ Lead a team within a larger organization

❑ Inspire and influence team members (without a supervisory role)

❑ Orchestrate, organize or support the activities of others

❑ Invent/design new products or services that benefit _____

❑ Set strategy and/or address big picture or urgent situations

❑ Get deep "in the weeds" and/or address technical or tactical issues

❑ Train, teach, coach, mentor or otherwise communicate with others

❑ Transform organizational culture or improve/streamline processes

❑ Keep an organization "on track" and/or out of trouble and/or manage risk

❑ Resolve disputes or complaints

❑ Market the organization and/or create and close on sales opportunities

❑ Analyze data to gain insights and support organizational goals

❑ Other _____

_____

_____

What interests me most from the above or other contributions I could make is:

_____

_____

_____

_____

The following aspects of a job are most important to me (rank or check your priorities):

Job Specifics

___ **Compensation:**

Current Base _____   Current Bonus/Incentives _____

Target Base _____   Target Bonus/Incentives _____

Minimum Total Compensation Sought and Details _____

___ **People/Environment** (list specifics or see below)

___ **Geographical location** (where?)

___ **Travel** (how much and where? no travel?)

___ **Short commute or ability to work from home**

___ **Health benefits and perks** (details: _____)

I am willing to work as follows, in exchange for the above:

___ "whatever it takes"

___ late nights but no weekends

___ full-time with flexible schedule

___ part-time

___ other _____

___ depends on the role (details: _____)

Intangibles

- ❑ Being respected

- ❑ Being creative

- ❑ Being social

- ❑ Feeling inspired

- ❑ Truly enjoying my work

- ❑ Experiencing excitement and activity

- ❑ Feeling a sense of completion and closure

- ❑ Having time for introspection and thinking

- ❑ Solving challenging intellectual problems

- ❑ Making a contribution to the world, my country or my community

- ❑ Advancing my field or making discoveries

- ❑ Mentoring and/or making sure others are heard

- ❑ Being part of a team or working collaboratively

- ❑ Having clear directions from management on goals

- ❑ Working independently or autonomously

- ❑ Working with people who are like and think like me

- ❑ Being exposed to diversity, other cultures and/or beliefs

- ❑ Helping people directly (hands-on)

- ❑ Working with children (or another group _____)

- ❑ Working in a humor-filled or laid-back environment

- ❑ Working in an achievement-oriented environment

❑   Variety among the workday or across days and months

❑   Stability and/or regularity

❑   Ability to do X (write, speak, research, be outdoors, work with my hands, etc.)

X is _____

❑   Knowing my work will or could make a long-term contribution

❑   Knowing I have the flexibility to retire or downshift my career at age _____

❑   Other _____

_____

Tradeoffs I am ready and/or willing to make:

_____

_____

Deal breakers (i.e., what I will not accept as a professional) and other negatives:

_____

_____

_____

_____

Insights I have gained from this unit

Changes (if any) I plan to make in my professional life:

UNIT 4 - SKILLS

Congratulations! You have exhibited the patience and perseverance – two great skills – to complete the first three units and arrive here.

In this unit, we are still taking an expansive approach as we think creatively about your personal value proposition. However, we also now have the end game in mind: what skills would be most applicable to the type of career that you are seeking to create for yourself?

To keep our minds open while we get more specific, we will take a top-down approach to skills. Rather than simply looking to the needs of the market and a particular job description to which you have applied or could apply to derive your strongest skills, try to be open to the broader universe of skills – including those that may apply as your role, field and world evolves over time, and others you may not have considered – and then narrow it down.

This unit has four distinct parts: (1) we start by creating an ideal job description that speaks to your strongest skills; (2) we then canvass top skills that are needed across virtually any profession and those that are highly transferable across roles; (3) adding to this skill list, we review specific examples of high-level substantive (hard) and intangible (soft) skills that could play into someone's value proposition in a specific field or career path; and (4) we finish the unit with a look at skill gaps and how to fill them.

Once you evaluated your skills holistically, you are in a better position to consider them in the context of a hypothetical or actual job search, business development campaign or request for internal advancement or lateral movement.

It is crucial that you are honest with yourself about what skills are your strengths, neither overvaluing nor undervaluing what you offer. You may be tempted to rate yourself high on soft skills that relate to emotional intelligence, for example, even if you are not good at reading others' verbal or visual cues or anticipating their needs. You also may be tempted to rate yourself low on skills that are actually some of your greatest assets. If you have any doubt whether a certain skill is a true strength, here are some ways that you can evaluate your abilities:

1) List examples of times you have exhibited the skill. The better examples that you can construct – assuming you have had sufficient work experience to support a skill – the more likely that a skill is one of your top strengths.

   Note: If you have not had sufficient work experience to support a skill, it may be that you have a nascent talent rather than being competent in the area. For example, you may be very collaborative by nature but have consistently found yourself in environments that value individual contributions. Alternatively, you may have become skilled in an area through means other than work (e.g., study or volunteer work), and if so you can draw on these experiences as well.

2) Ask others (whose opinions you trust and who have had a chance to witness you in action) to evaluate you on your strongest skills. If it is helpful, you can share the lists below (reproduced at www.annemariesegal.com/worksheets) and ask them to evaluate your top skills.

3) Read more in-depth articles about those skills you would rate as your strongest and compare the commentary or examples to your own skills.

Note: On the third point, Harvard Business Review (hbr.org) is a great resource, online and in print, on virtually any career or business skill you may encounter. Search online for "Harvard Business Review" or "HBR" and the name of the specific skill. Harvard Business Review also has a host of general articles that cut across a range of skills.

Deconstructing Larger Skill Sets

Some of you may find that your strongest skills come to mind more easily in the context of "what you do" professionally, rather than as individual components involved in each task.

Here are some diverse examples of functional areas (and there are many more) through which you could add value to an organization:

- Strategy
- Deal-Making
- Product Development
- Marketing
- Financial and/or Risk Management
- Recruiting
- Training
- Legal

If you are more familiar with thinking about your contributions in that context, this unit can help you to breakdown your functional areas into specific skills.

For example, if "what you do" is to keep your organization compliant and out of legal trouble, what are you actually doing on a day-to-day basis? For example, are you researching or otherwise gathering information, evaluating risk, building relationships with and influencing executives and others, training employees, writing policies, taking or supporting disciplinary actions and/or negotiating with regulatory authorities?

If you are in marketing, by contrast, are you clarifying stakeholder objectives, identifying relevant markets, creating a platform for a product or service, designing social media campaigns, writing copy, running focus groups and/or taking surveys?

Each of these activities involves a transferable skill that may be key to your current or a future role. Once you have clarified what your role entails, you can then connect each of those individual activities to the role-specific skills below.

"What I Do" professionally (currently or historically) and the skills that are involved:

If I am changing careers or advancing within my field, what I expect or want to do next:

If I wrote my own job description from scratch (or, alternatively, a bullet point checklist of the challenges I wish to take on in my career and strengths I need to do that), it would say:

A. SKILLS SETS

There are certain proficiencies that pull from various skill sets, represent your main strengths and are highly strategic and transferrable among roles. The term "transferrable" means that skills are not only applicable to one career or field but are relevant to other roles. Both hard skills and soft skills can be transferrable, depending on the individual skill.

Note: While the phrase "transferrable talents" has not caught on in the same way as transferrable skills, a set of talents would be just as transferrable.

To help you think about your skill sets, I am including here some lists that I created. They are not exhaustive, but it will get you started in the right direction.

I suggest you conduct research to learn more about any set of skills that you seek to expand further or wish to have more information to consider. As I mentioned above, HBR is a great resource for this purpose, and there are others online and on the library shelves.

Ranking of Skills Based on Your Seniority, Individual Role and Other Factors

While you may possess dozens of skills, focus first on the ones that are most helpful for your current or target role(s) and consider your other skills as complementary.

CEOs, for example, needs to know how to sell their ideas and the products and services of their companies. They also should be great mentors, risk takers and risk managers. But not all CEOs have the same set of sharp skills in their toolboxes, and their need to differentiate themselves is as strong (or stronger) than that of anyone else. In addition, depending on where their skills lie, they may find different markets that would prove a better fit.

In smaller companies, of course, CEOs will need a much broader range of robust skills to be successful. Nonetheless, they should honestly rank and seek feedback so they can assess how these strengths can help them grow their own careers and the careers of their employees (which, by extension, helps the business thrive).

Note: The category headers below provide some order to this unit, but they should not be read as definitive divisions of job types or skills.

High-Level (and Highly Transferable) Skills

Leadership Skills

Vision	Communication
Innovation/Creativity/Curiosity	Influence/Political Capital
Strategic Thinking and Planning	Mentoring Ability
Negotiation	Board/Stakeholder Management

Other High-Level Skills

Grasp of P&L/Financial Analysis	Research/Due Diligence
Project Management	Marketing Ability
Risk Management	Sales Ability
Organizational Skills	Flexibility
Collaboration	Customer-Service Orientation
Team-Player Orientation	Results-Orientation
Entrepreneurial Skills	Resiliency
Comfort with Risk-Taking	Risk Management Skills

From the above or other skills, choose your top four and complete the blanks below.

Note: If you check that a skill comes naturally to you – and for this purpose I mean that you are "at your best" or "in your element" when exercising this skill, even if it took some effort to acquire the skill – reflect on these answers again when you turn to the chapter on talents.

Top Skill #1: _____

This skill comes naturally to me: ___ Absolutely   ___ To some degree   ___ Not at all

I exhibit this skill: ___ Always   ___ Often   ___ Sometimes   ___ Seldom

I have really needed this skill when: _____

_____

_____

I have demonstrated my strength in this skill when: _____

_____

_____

This skill is important in my career because: _____

_____

_____

Top Skill #2: _____

This skill comes naturally to me: ___ Absolutely ___ To some degree ___ Not at all

I exhibit this skill: ___ Always ___ Often ___ Sometimes ___ Seldom

I have really needed this skill when: _____

_____

_____

I have demonstrated my strength in this skill when: _____

_____

_____

This skill is important in my career because: _____

_____

_____

Top Skill #3: _____

This skill comes naturally to me: ___ Absolutely ___ To some degree ___ Not at all

I exhibit this skill: ___ Always ___ Often ___ Sometimes ___ Seldom

I have really needed this skill when: _____

_____

_____

I have demonstrated my strength in this skill when: _____

_____

_____

This skill is important in my career because: _____

_____

_____

Top Skill #4: _____

This skill is a also talent of mine: ___ Absolutely ___ To some degree ___ Not at all

I exhibit this skill: ___ Always ___ Often ___ Sometimes ___ Seldom

I have really needed this skill when: _____

_____

_____

I have demonstrated my strength in this skill when: _____

_____

_____

This skill is important in my career because: _____

_____

_____

The Multi-Faceted Skill Set of Leadership

Thousands of books, courses and other resources have been created that attempt to define leadership – one of the key skills one can possess, along with communication skills – and I cannot pretend to offer a full definition here. On a practical level, one leads through setting organizational or departmental goals (often in collaboration with other leaders) and then bringing together and motivating a team to achieve those goals. This contrasts with making individual contributions: as a leader you pave and guide the way for others. In many ways, leadership encompasses a range of other skills, and those that comprise your leadership style define the type of a leader you are.

> Note: If you are a CEO or otherwise "always a leader" in your current role, what are your greatest leadership accomplishments? If you are just starting or returning to your career, what leadership opportunities have you gained through school, volunteering or otherwise? What tangible results can you articulate that you have achieved?

I have exhibited my greatest leadership skills when (continues on the following page):

1) _____

_____

_____

2) _____

_____

_____

3) _____

_____

_____

Personality Traits that Double as Skills

The following personality traits also represent real-world skills that are sought after in many roles and, as long as one already has or can develop some talent for them, can be nurtured and grown with attention and effort.

Even a sense of humor – one that draws other people to you and increases your ability to "get things done" with your team, clients and those far afield in the organization – is a skill you can grow once you see the value in it. Think about which traits below you have grown into top skills and the importance each may have in your career.

Decisiveness	Patience
Pragmatism	Diplomacy
"Tough Skin"	Calm/Groundedness
Sense of Humor	Work Ethic
Credibility	Motivation of Others
Integrity	Empathy
Good Judgment	Resiliency
Self-Motivation	Grit

> **Note**: These traits are variations of others (e.g., integrity and ethics are interrelated), and this is by no means an exhaustive list. When describing your skills, use the terms that best fit your field and situation.

From the prior list or other traits of your choosing, choose your top four and complete the exercises on the following page. You are welcome to vet and rank more skills and slip those notes into the book.

Top Trait/Skill #1: _____

This skill comes naturally to me: ___ Absolutely ___ To some degree ___ Not at all

I exhibit this skill: ___ Always ___ Often ___ Sometimes ___ Seldom

I have really needed this skill when: _____

_____

_____

I have demonstrated my strength in this skill when: _____

_____

_____

This skill is important in my career because: _____

_____

_____

Top Trait/Skill #2: _____

This skill comes naturally to me: ___ Absolutely ___ To some degree ___ Not at all

I exhibit this skill: ___ Always ___ Often ___ Sometimes ___ Seldom

I have really needed this skill when: _____

_____

_____

I have demonstrated my strength in this skill when: _____

_____

_____

This skill is important in my career because: _____

_____

_____

Top Trait/Skill #3: _____

This skill comes naturally to me: ___ Absolutely   ___ To some degree   ___ Not at all

I exhibit this skill: ___ Always ___ Often ___ Sometimes ___ Seldom

I have really needed this skill when: _____

_____

_____

I have demonstrated my strength in this skill when: _____

_____

_____

This skill is important in my career because: _____

_____

_____

Top Trait/Skill #4: _____

This skill comes naturally to me: ___ Absolutely   ___ To some degree   ___ Not at all

I exhibit this skill: ___ Always ___ Often ___ Sometimes ___ Seldom

I have really needed this skill when: _____

_____

_____

I have demonstrated my strength in this skill when: _____

_____

_____

This skill is important in my career because: _____

_____

_____

Recapping Your Top Transferrable Skills

Summing up, among the skills and traits above (or others), my greatest are:

_____

_____

_____

_____

_____

_____

C. ROLE-SPECIFIC SKILLS

In addition to the general skills discussed above, of course, there are skills that serve you quite well in specific roles but may not be highly transferrable.

As an example, below is a long (but not complete) list of skills that a chef could have, including for sake of a comprehensive review some duplications from the high-level skills above. I chose this profession to highlight because most of us are generally familiar with cooking, but we may not all have thought about everything that can go into making a great (or even an average) chef. Not all chefs possess all of the skills below, although many great chefs hold a large subset of the skills in the lists below, or if they hold a smaller subset, they probably hold *the right ones* for whatever role they have.

We must not forget the larger context, of course. None of a chef's skills would matter if the food did not taste good, look appealing on the plate and pass relevant health standards (regulatory and otherwise). A chef's talent – and I will discuss talents more in the next chapter – is to bring together a creation that is larger than the sum of its parts.

Hard (Substantive) Skills:

- Kitchen Skills
- Culinary Expertise
- Recipe Creation
- Menu Management
- Quality Control
- Inventory Management
- Food Shopping and Pricing
- Cleanliness/ Food Safety
- Regulatory/Health Code Knowledge

- Restaurant, Hotel and/or Catering Experience
- Supervisory Experience
- Human Resource Management
- Project Management
- Business Savvy
- Marketing/Sales Ability
- Heat Control

Within the kitchen skills above, there are many subcategories, including as examples:

- using knives (knife skills)
- baking
- cooking meat (braising, barbequing, etc.)
- boning and cooking fish (grilling, poaching, etc.)
- making a vinaigrette
- employing sous vide techniques

Other skills in the list above can be broken down further as well.

For the skill of "culinary expertise," the corresponding *talent* may be a "knack for cooking" or "attuned palate." Similarly, other skills above and below are ones for which a chef may demonstrate a natural talent or need to learn despite a lack of intuition in the relevant area.

Soft (Interpersonal) Skills:

- Attention to Detail
- Speed
- Ability to Multitask
- Passion
- Creativity/Innovation
- Consistency
- Strategic Thinking
- Leadership
- Negotiation Skills
- Communication Skills
- Networking Skills
- Team-Player Orientation
- Problem Solving
- Decisiveness
- Efficiency
- Organization (mis en place)
- Systematic Approach
- Sense of Urgency
- Patience
- Grace under Pressure
- Discipline

- Empathy/Mentorship Ability
- Pragmatism
- Honesty
- Health/Health-Focus
- Uncompromising Taste
- Economy
- Loyalty/Commitment
- Visual/Design-Orientation
- Resiliency
- Physical Stamina
- Physical Dexterity
- Work Ethic
- Tough Skin
- Sense of Humor
- Flexibility
- Time Management Skills
- Conflict Resolution Skills

Transferable Skills a Chef Might Possess

From the first list (of hard skills) above:

1) Business savvy, marketing, supervisory expertise and project management are all highly transferrable skills across a range of industries and roles.

2) Quality control or inventory management could be positioned as transferrable skills to the extent that they involve attention to detail, or they could be highly transferrable if the chef was targeting a new market with a need for those skills (e.g., retail).

3) Recipe creation, on the other hand, is less transferrable as it is more specific.

To some degree, any skill is transferable as long as you can envision and articulate to your audience how it applies to your target role. Recipe creation, for example, may be analogous to other forms of invention and written communication (depending on the chef's actual involvement in the process). That said, some skills are easier to pitch as transferrable to new roles than others, because they are either more directly related to the new role or would represent a "smaller mental leap" from the old to new role.

My takeaways from the above are:

_____

_____

_____

Skills that Give You an Edge

In addition to traditional hard and soft skills for any given profession, certain of us may have an "edge" that can change the dynamic of our careers if we wish to incorporate it and find a way to connect that edge with the needs of the market. This edge may come from our work experience or our personal interests.

Here are some diverse examples of an edge one may have:

- a COO candidate may be a former recruiter (and have a great eye for acquiring new talent) or may have lived abroad for a number of years before returning to the U.S. (and possess a keen understanding of cultural differences among a diverse, international workforce);

- a financial advisor working with special needs families may have faced similar challenges as a parent or witnessed them through contact with a close friend's child (and be able to demonstrate compassion, relate to their experience and create an effective financial plan);

- an architect or real estate developer may have a LEED certification (and a demonstrated interest in environmentally friendly construction); or

- a marketing officer may be an active participant in social media platforms such as Twitter or Instagram (and have great instincts for achieving higher market penetration for the firm or organization's products and services).

The idea behind an edge is that it is not a skill that would generally be held by most individuals holding a specific role, but it nonetheless is highly relevant to certain opportunities, if the right opportunity is sought out.

Examples of an Edge a Chef Might Have

- Highly Entrepreneurial
- Trained under [Name of Famous Chef] or managed [Name of Famous Restaurant]
- Storyteller
- Teacher
- Chemistry or food science background
- Farming background
- Nutritionist background or certification
- Fluency in one or more foreign languages
- Extensive knowledge of a "foreign" (to the local environment) or fusion cuisine
- Sommelier training
- Slow food or other activism
- Extensive knowledge of allergies or other dietary needs
- Industry or other professional background (e.g., lawyer-turned-chef)
- Media or social media background

Your Own Role-Specific Skills

Now it is time for you to create your own list of role-specific skill sets. You may wish to refer back to the beginning of this unit where I listed some sources that you can use to facilitate your list.

Note: If you are in the midst of a career change and have fewer points of reference, you can print out some job descriptions and use those in combination with your personal wisdom and what you have learned in this book, but please only if you can do that without becoming emotionally charged – positively or negatively – by the content of the job descriptions. They are not, for this exercise, roles to which you are actually applying (so don't stress about whether or not you will be successful at landing them). They are points of reference.

Hard Skills:

_____

_____

_____

_____

_____

Soft Skills:

_____

_____

_____

_____

_____

D. ADDRESSING GAPS

If you have gaps in certain sets of skills that you would otherwise like to incorporate into your personal value proposition, you have three main options: **(1) decide you are not qualified** for the roles you would like and decline to pursue those roles, (2) **consider whether you have analogous experience** that will bridge the gap while you acquire the skills or (3) **find a way to accelerate your skill acquisition**.

The first could not only rob you of many opportunities but will also deprive the workforce and world of your skills and talents. That said, you may determine the gap is too great or that you do not have the motivation at this point in time to close it. The latter two strategies (using analogies and accelerating skill acquisition) can be employed simultaneously.

To decide if you have analogous experience, you may need to break a skill set down into its component parts. For example, if you want to move into a role but do not have any sales experience, how can you demonstrate you hold the bundle of skills that go into what we generally refer to as "sales skills"? Here are some ideas:

1) Communication
2) Passion for/Knowledge of Product or Service
3) Client-Service Orientation
4) Persuasiveness
5) Storytelling
6) Negotiation Skills
7) Persistence (Follow-Up)
8) Problem-Solving

If you can demonstrate that you have exhibited these more specific skills in aspects of your career that are (or seem to be, at first glance) unrelated to sales, it will go a long way toward demonstrating that you would be a great salesperson.

Separately, you may need to demonstrate your ability to utilize a client-relationship management (CRM) software to keep track of all of your interactions with prospects and clients. In fact, some companies require that salespeople use these tools to record and take notes for every meeting or call, because they have found that keeping consistent records increases their overall sales revenue. In addition to not having sales experience, you may have never used CRM and may not even know how it works or what it is. (Hint: Look up what you don't know!) Yet you may have used Excel or other software, and you could show that you could quickly get up to speed with CRM. Another skill that you would need to demonstrate to show your aptitude to learn and use CRM would be attention to detail.

As a second strategy, in order to jumpstart this new career (which could be a "true sales" role or one that involves sales, such as a financial advisor), you may wish to take sales training. However, if you can move into a role on the basis of your analogous skills – by understanding what the role requires and demonstrating that you meet the requirements – you may be able to move into the new field first and then take the training afterwards. In addition to saving yourself the risk of investing time to learn a new field without an immediate application and losing the chance to invest that time in something else, you may be able to complete your training at the company's expense rather than your own.

Skills versus Interests Gap

While we have talked about a skills gap, and that is easy to understand, it is also possible to have an interest gap.

If you are applying for a job at Facebook or Twitter, for example, and you have no interest in using the products and services each supports and or how social media is changing our global communications, that is an interests gap. Still, you may find the rest of the job description appealing, have other skills, be hired and make some great contributions to the company. As time wears on, however, you may realize that you are not working toward a common organizational goal and are likely to become disengaged with your work.

On the other hand, if you love the idea of Facebook and Twitter and how they are transforming the world, but you do not offer skills that match either company needs (or, at least, the needs of the roles that appeal to you), that is a skills gap.

When faced with an interests gap, there are ways to grow your interest in certain areas, but to some degree you naturally gravitate towards certain things and not others. You may also lose interest in an area because you have become "burned out" on it. This can happen before you are aware of why you have lost interest, especially if you feel particularly loyal to a certain organization or cause.

When faced with a skills gap, you need to ask yourself if you have talents and interest in the area, how much time and effort it would require to obtain such skills and whether you would reap the benefit of such skills at a level that makes the investment worth it. This is another iteration of the ROI-approach discussed in Unit 3.

Reviewing Your Skills Gaps

If you have the opportunity and motivation to improve your ability to communicate – as probably 100% of us could – this skill reigns supreme in just about any role. If relevant, consider adding it to the list below and flesh out specifics (including the type of communication you could improve and in which contexts).

If you are very savvy about skills already, you may wish to address very specific gaps, such as areas within your strengths that could be refined to allow for even greater versatility and raise your comfort level across the skill set.

How to Grow Your Skills

To give you insight into how you might grow a skill, consider a senior candidate (let's call her Susan) who has led teams of 10+ individuals for a number of years but is now pivoting into or hoping to advance to a role that generally requires someone to lead teams of 100+ individuals. Leadership is one of her strengths, but she may face the challenge of showing she can credibly raise her game to the next level.

Susan's best strategy is to bolster all the knowledge and support she can for her argument that she is a convincing candidate for this increased level of responsibility. She could, for example, canvass other leaders who currently have larger teams to learn how to tackle the differences of scale, enroll in a targeted leadership program and read relevant books or other resources. She could also chair a large-scale event for a non-profit (which could give her exposure to management of a large team and round out this skill).

Most importantly, what Susan needs to do is identify the elements of change that she will encounter by going from 10+ to 100+ reports and then be able to address how she will adapt and thrive in the new role. Her people management, time management, delegation and other skills, for example, may need to be retooled. If she can pro-actively speak to these adaptations, she will have a stronger value proposition than a similar candidate who cannot.

Top Skills for my current or target field or roles (that I do not possess or need to improve):

Skill Gap #1:

_____

_____

My strategies to grow this skill:

_____

_____

_____

_____

_____

Skill Gap #2:

_____

_____

My strategies to grow this skill:

_____

_____

_____

_____

_____

Skill Gap #3:

_____

_____

My strategies to grow this skill:

_____

_____

_____

_____

_____

_____

Skill Gap #4:

_____

_____

My strategies to grow this skill:

_____

_____

_____

_____

_____

_____

Further Note About Gaps

For my readers who tend to feel anxiety about gaps in their skills, remember that I gave you three strategies on page 69 above to address gaps. It would behoove you to use them.

What you should <u>not</u> do, by contrast, is waste time and energy <u>worrying</u> about how you are perceived due to your gaps. You can only control your own actions and efforts, not reactions to them. Save your energy for something that you actually <u>can</u> change, like adding to your skills so that they increase your personal value proposition.

Yes, it may be that you discover upon your due diligence (in Unit 6) that the gap is too large to pivot into a field you had hoped to target and that you cannot reasonably make the investment to close it (or simply do not have "what it takes"). Yet worrying will not solve that problem or any other. Instead, you need to dust yourself off and get a new strategy.

E. CONCLUSION

Key Takeaways About My Skills:

My Next Steps (If Any) Regarding My Skills:

UNIT 5 - TALENTS

Are you in touch with your talents? `

I recognize that readers of this book may fall into two extremes. First, there are the ones who are very aware of their talents, as they have already been using these talents at a very high level regularly. Second, there are readers who may know they have certain talents but are struck with some variation of imposter syndrome and think that they *could not possibly* actually be talented at these things, it is only an illusion. There will also be readers who are at some mid-point on that scale or vacillate between these extremes.

Regardless of which type of reader you are, we can all get more in touch with our talents. If you have been consistently rewarded for using one aspect of your talent base, you may have lost touch with other talents you possess. Similarly, if you have had an overarching talent that you can no longer exercise due to more recent mental, physical or other limitations, it could be time to explore other talents that can emerge to take its place.

The wisdom of nurturing diverse talents is why you see, for example, very talented doctors who swim, lawyers who make pottery, mathematicians who play guitar, venture capitalists who surf and the like. This cross-nurturing of talents does not need to be related to art, music or a sport (for those who are not engaged in either as their "regular" job), although often they are, since art, music and sport can stimulate other parts of the body and brain. Those who are working artists, musicians and athletes may follow the opposite path, bringing in related left-brained activities, such as operating a dance company, theater or recording studio.

The use of diverse talents can also draw on related or complementary areas of one's main career, such as doctors who see patients and also pioneer the advancement of a hospital's medical informatics (combining healthcare and information technology), lawyers who write fiction with plots turning on legal issues, mathematicians who sit on corporate boards of directors or venture capitalists who launch non-profit organizations. Of course, these individuals may hold talents in multiple areas and consistently look for new talents to weave into a talent braid that is stronger than any single strand.

Talents versus Skills

We should take a moment to stop and revisit the similarities and differences between talents and skills as I use these terms here. As I defined these earlier in the book, **skills** are concrete, substantive proficiencies one holds, has achieved or can achieve through focused efforts and dedication and **talents** are what comes naturally or easily to someone (whether innately or through repeated exposure).

To some degree, "repeated exposure" is similar to the training or experience that one would undertake to grow a skill, and talents can be latent and need some focused efforts to reinvigorate. So can we always tell the difference between a talent or a skill?

Sometimes it is obvious; other times it is unclear. What <u>is</u> clear is that we sometimes develop skills in areas in which we have very little talent, and despite our best efforts to become experts in those areas, we cannot seem to close the gap. Attention to detail is a perfect and versatile example of one of these areas that could be both a talent and a skill. To the extent that we all need some level of attention to detail, we have all developed some skills (or coping mechanisms) to achieve that. Yet some of us absorb the details without exerting great effort, while others need to force themselves to do so. Further, we may have attention to detail in some areas of our life but are oblivious in other areas.

You probably have encountered people who take a red pen to everything, even when you have not asked for help, versus those who make multiple grammatical errors despite proofreading a three-paragraph email five times. We might be inclined to assume that the former individuals have strong attention to detail while the latter do not, but remember that other skills (grammar and language fluency) also come into play. Further, someone could be a very detailed-oriented person but have trouble spelling for neurological reasons. I worked for many years with one individual who could not spell to save her life, but she could put her finger on every single document she had drafted and remember every deal she had closed over a 20+ year paralegal career.

There are also times when a skill has not ripened into a talent and may never do so. This is an important point for all of us and especially for those in career transition. Remember my example of the chef above. If you have every single skill on the list but do not have a knack for cooking – meaning, you have given yourself sufficient time for that talent to bloom, under the right set of conditions, and it has not – you may locate employment as a chef but will not be poised to attain true career satisfaction. This is the crux of the distinction between talents and skills. You need skills to succeed, but talent is like the glue that keeps the skills together.

Talents versus Interests

Talents are similar to interests as well, although again distinct. Although they generally overlap, as the things that comes easily to us are also what we like doing, we can have an interest but not a talent or vice versa.

For a real world example, imagine that a friend convinces you to try out for a local musical, and you grudgingly say yes, even though you have never sung or acted on a stage in your life. To everyone's surprise, including your own, you get the lead. After many weeks of rehearsing, you have a few performances. While you forget a line once and sound a bit off-key in the first scene, you recover. Your performance is amazing. The audience is enthralled.

Your friend says, "wow you have a real talent for acting. You should do more of this." His opinion is echoed by critics and others who have seen the show.

You are now at a crossroads. You have discovered a new **talent**, but do you have the **interest** and motivation to acquire more **skills** and become a versatile actor able to successfully portray a range of characters in many different roles? Should you consider whether you have latent talents for other activities you may not have known, including ones that could have a greater – or different – market, like public speaking?

New things have tried that I did not expect to be successful but was pleasantly surprised:

What I can draw out of those experiences:

Do Talents Always Come Naturally?

We may never know the full degree to which talents are innate or learned, and there likely will continue to be discussions and scientific evidence backing up one theory or another. The prevailing wisdom seems to be that while we can achieve an appreciable level of success in almost any area with consistent practice – thousands upon thousands of hours – we are born with proclivities that increase our range and aptitude in certain areas more than others.

For our purposes here today, we are not looking backward at "what you could have become" if you had practiced more in math and science, foreign languages, musical instruments, sports or other activities as a child. Since we cannot change the past, what your innate talents might have been if properly channeled is irrelevant for our work here. Instead, what we are most interested in learning is what talents you have now (whether or not you have always had them) and can exercise from this moment forward.

Talents I already <u>know</u> that I have are:

I also have very good instincts about:

If you don't feel satisfied with your list, your next task is to uncover what you are missing. Talents are something we often do not notice about ourselves. Why? By definition, if we are talented at something, it comes relatively easily for us. We often discount our abilities to do things that come easily, because we assume (falsely) that they also come easily to everyone else. In addition, if we have been told not to brag about ourselves, we may have lost touch with talents in our efforts to please others or fit in.

To the extent that you are an astute observer of human behavior (and have already surmised what makes you unique from others) or you have received positive and consistent feedback, you may already be familiar your talents. To harness observation, take a look at what others call up as struggles and decide if you may have a hidden talent that enables you to soar in the same type of situation. To become more aware of feedback, listen for phrases such as:

You are a master of….

How do you do that…?

You have great instincts for…

Where did you ever learn…?

You have such a knack for….

Did I ever tell you how much I appreciate your…?

If we listen for these phrases and hear them enough times from credible sources (who are focused on our needs, not their own), we know that we are on to something.

The above phrases remind me that I have become known for:

We are back to brainstorming mode here. Feel free to list in the exercises above any talent, from speaking to crowds and raising money for charities to keeping your desk organized and deflecting comments from a toxic boss. The idea is to turn on the creative part of your brain that connects you with your intuition, so you can become more aware of more of your talents and bring them to the fore in your daily life.

Speaking of intuition, if you review what you wrote in the early units about work activities that do not feel like "work" and other times you are in the flow, you may have uncovered some of your talents there.

In fact, go through your entire list of interests and skills. If you consider what you obsess about, do any talents emerge? And if you do not obsess about anything, that is certainly a talent as well! What about current mentors or childhood heroes? Other insights?

Don't be shy or restrained about your talents. Let go of the voice that says, "you are not *that* good…." You can prioritize later. Just get it on the page.

Tasks I do not delegate because I enjoy them, do a great job and can finish them quickly and efficiently (talent alert!):

What I can find in books or online about "top talents" that reveal even more of my talents:

Hidden Talents

In writing this section of the book, I am reminded of clients who exhibit talents that are obvious to me – as a neutral third party – but oblivious to them. Some examples include those who present well, exude leadership, negotiate with the best of them or consistently "see around corners" to troubleshoot problems that may arise.

Not everyone sees his or her own talents clearly, as I mentioned above. In fact, I often hear, "I thought everyone did that," when I talk to clients about their talents. If you are good at something, it comes easily, and you may forget that it may not be as easy for others.

If you believe that you are missing some of your talents or not connecting with your greatest ones, this may be the perfect time to poll five or ten friends, family, supervisors, employees and/or colleagues (i.e., a 360-degree review). Tell them you are doing a self-assessment – you can even tell them about this book, I won't mind! – to help you grow your career, and that you are happy to return the favor. Make sure to record their answers.

Lost Talents

Sometimes we have a talent early in life and then, because it is not nurtured, we seem to lose it. For example, you may have had a talent for numbers, painting, debating, entrepreneurship or another area, and you lost track of it based on feedback you received and other opportunities that became available.

Maybe you were always the kid who had a lemonade stand or was trying to make money through yard work, household chores or even more skilled labor (such as fixing computers), but then you moved into a career that paid well but did not grow your entrepreneurial muscles. Now you wish to launch your own business, and you are wondering if you have what it takes to make it a success.

If you have any latent or lost talents that you want to recover and have the motivation to do so, the first step is to know what you are missing (e.g., refer to Reconnecting with My Younger Self on page 29 above) and the second is to exercise those talent muscles again.

Talents I want to reconnect with:

My commitment to connecting with those talents (with 10 as the highest):

1   2   3   4   5   6   7   8   9   10

What I can do to make that happen (actionable steps and timeline):

Talents in Context

Everything can be viewed as a strength or a weakness depending on what is called for in one's own career. Consider the following list of very concrete talents, some complementary and others that could run contrary to each other (or would need to be compartmentalized and run on parallel tracks):

- Asking pivotal questions
- Making decisions
- Reserving judgment
- Leaving no stone unturned
- Prioritizing tasks
- Arguing persuasively for one's side
- Considering multiple points of view
- Bringing the major players to the table
- Accounting for minority voices

- Exercising authority
- Influencing without authority
- Sniffing out inconsistencies
- Allowing for occasional contradictions
- Staying on task
- Generating ideas
- Testing ideas
- Executing ideas
- Properly allocating resources
- Analyzing (taking things or ideas apart)
- Synthesizing (bringing things or ideas together)
- Multitasking
- Monotasking
- Collaborating
- Compartmentalizing
- Staying the course under criticism
- Knowing when to adjust course with new input
- Rebounding from hurdles or failures
- Managing a heavy workload
- Focusing not on workload, but on results'
- Appreciating nuances
- Getting to closure

After reading the above list, I realize I also have talent(s) for:

More About My Talents

Top talents that will play into my growing career goals:

Top talents that could take me in an entirely new direction:

Talents that (at this point) are not highly valued in my current career path:

Challenges, negativity or stumbling blocks that may prevent me from exercising my talents:

How I can overcome the blocks:

Other ways I can grow or cross-nurture my talents:

<u>Themes I Recognize About My Talents:</u>

PART 2:

MARKET NEEDS

UNIT 6 – UNDERSTANDING MARKET NEEDS

In Part 1, we discussed your needs and strengths (rather than market needs) as means to gauge your end of your personal value proposition. Jumping directly to an external point of reference could easily cause us to miss what we uniquely have to offer the world while absorbed in the search for the next job, client or other professional match.

Yet we must, of course, assess our value propositions in terms of how we can serve the market (again, serving the "market" means serving people, even if the term sounds depersonalized). In this unit, as a starting point, we are focused on market needs.

To reflect our revised focus, let's reverse the order of the personal value proposition equation:

Market Needs + Your Strengths + Your Priorities =

Your Personal Value Proposition

Philosophically speaking, by reversing the PVP equation, we are not minimizing our own priorities and strengths but instead viewing them through the lens of market needs. Put another way, we are determining how to evaluate our needs in the service of the market and, by extension, identifying the right market to meet both sets of needs.

As you know, you can have all the skills and talents in the world, but if the market does not value what you offer, you will not be gainfully employed (in an appropriate role). Fortunately, like no time in history, we have access to more markets than ever before.

Market Needs for Your Strengths

At the most basic level, you are a fit for a role if you have the skills. If an organization is forward-thinking, it may value nascent talents more than present skills, on the assumption that you can learn new skills but you cannot create talent where it does not exist. On certain occasions, interests and/or values are prized. As an obvious example, for a role at a dog food company, it may help if you like dogs (especially if they are a dog-friendly workplace).

The same holds true for many organizations that create other products and services that fulfill human interests. A number of my clients have professed to be "agnostic" with respect to what a company does, in an effort to keep their options open. While this does demonstrate versatility, it can also backfire, making you a less compelling candidate because you come across as too polite or lacking in personality.

If your interests are aligned with those of your market, you are likely a step ahead of the game because you will feel invigorated by new developments in the field, advance more quickly up the professional food chain, stay longer in each individual job and avoid or mitigate career speed bumps during layoffs and downturns. In fact, having interests, values and preferences that align with a work culture and job (or client) goes a long way toward being the right "fit," that elusive quality that everyone looks for most when hiring.

When I say that your interests play into your fit with an organization, I do not mean that companies expect everyone to engage in group-think and all like the same movies, food and jokes. However, they do want their employees to have compatible and complementary personalities and values, and these both play out in your interests. If your favorite activities are rock-climbing and scuba diving, you are likely to be adventurous yet meticulous (as well as physically fit). If you are a news junkie, you are likely concerned about macro-events and someone who processes information very quickly. If you volunteer at your local food bank, you are likely someone who will demonstrate compassion and teamwork. **These are generalizations, but as we look to communicate our value, we must be aware of the "clues" that we project, because the right clues help build our credibility.**

Assessing Market Needs

If you have been actively engaged in the work of the prior units, you may come to this chapter with a burning question: how do I know which of my strengths are most valued by the market? This is, in fact, a key point of inquiry in this book.

In the case of employment, your assessment of market needs can come from (A) a specific job description and postings of similar jobs, (B) due diligence on the industry and the company (from its website, press and other sources), (C) informational interviews and (D) accumulated personal knowledge of what is sought by your industry, target organizations and roles which you have accumulated by being involved in the field or more generally, including an awareness of broadly transferrable skills (as discussed above in Unit 4).

Entrepreneurs can seek out similar data points, with their diligence, informational interviews and personal knowledge focused on their target client base.

The first three data points about market needs are not in order of priority; they are in order of how you might approach them chronologically. In other words, start with job descriptions and other due diligence, so you know what questions to ask in your informational interviews. The fourth data point, accumulated personal knowledge, is your filter to apply throughout the process and will help you gauge what due diligence to conduct. You should also revisit your personal knowledge – including gut instincts – at the end of the process, as you conduct the final analysis of market needs.

Data Points to Assess Market Needs

Job Descriptions
Due Diligence
Informational Interviews
Personal Knowledge

In Sections A through D below, I describe the four data points above in more detail and give you an opportunity to reflect on any information gaps. Then there are multiple worksheets available to aggregate the information for your current role (if any) and two additional target roles (for a transition or advancement). You may wish to refer to these sections again as you complete the worksheets.

Note: For business owners, job descriptions are a much smaller part of the analysis, although they may yield helpful information about client needs and gaps that can be filled through products and services.

A. JOB DESCRIPTIONS

How to Read a Job Description

To assess market needs for a particular position – your current or target role – you can start by reading the job description, if available. In addition, you can pull similar job descriptions for similar roles to compare and contrast, especially if the job description for your role is not particularly illustrative or detailed.

When I first started coaching, I was surprised how many job candidates (including senior executives) did not slow down and actually read job descriptions. I have now worked with hundreds of clients on job searches and value proposition development, and I have seen that quite a good number of them fail to comb through job descriptions line by line and word by word or fail, as a second step, to ask themselves what might emerge when they "read between the lines."

A competent job description not only recites the expectations for the job but also gives you insight into the culture of the employer, especially as you *compare it to other job descriptions* for similar roles. Some job descriptions hold very few keys about what a position entails, but others can be quite illustrative if you read them closely.

Here are two examples of insights from job descriptions:

- Entrepreneurial mindset

- Ability to work well under time constraints and to meet deadlines

I have had candidates sit in my office and tell me they want to leave a law firm, for example, because they do not want the pressure of business development. Yet when they show me a job description for an entrepreneurial role, and I ask them about it, they stick their heads in the sand. "Yes, I saw that. I guess it would be OK…."

"I guess it would be OK" is not a resounding vote on the entrepreneurial front; it is grudgingly entrepreneurial. If a role expects you to have the mindset of an entrepreneur and you do not have one. You may be <u>hired</u>, but you will nonetheless need to drum up the interest, courage and skills of an entrepreneur to be <u>successful</u>.

These two scenarios are not mutually exclusive. You can certainly be entrepreneurial without being motivated to generate clients as an attorney, wanting instead to generate other types of business with a different set of clients. In other words, you could be very bad at winning over law clients and very good at selling cookies (think Fortune 500 cookie company not bake sale, or think bake sale with an ability to scale).

Sometimes a disconnect arises because otherwise intelligent people do not stop to ask themselves basic questions, such as, "What does it mean to have an entrepreneurial mindset?" They are not reading word by word, and they are not using resources to get to the heart of the words on the page. They seem instead to distrust the job description (and, unknowingly, its author) and assume that they can either fake what they do not have or ignore what does not apply to them. Nothing is further from the truth. "Fake it until you make it" does not mean you should take on a long-term role that is not authentic to you. It means having the courage to imagine a life that is greater than the one you currently occupy and growing into the skills for which you already have talents. "Faking it" only works for taking leaps of faith in the right direction. It doesn't work for throwing darts blindfolded, which only results in one or more people getting hurt (including you).

The *Financial Times* (lexicon.ft.com) definition of individuals with an entrepreneurial mindset are those who:

- are often drawn to opportunities, innovation and new value creation;
- have an ability to take calculated risks; and
- can accept the realities of change and uncertainty.

We could drill down further and ask what each of these words mean (what is "new value creation?" what is a "calculated risk?"), and you are free to do so. The greater takeaway here is that if you are very risk-averse, do not like change, are not a people-person (see Units 2 and 3), prefer closure to options (see Unit 2) and generally like to have your days and weeks planned out in advance without a lot of disruption, then entrepreneurship is not the job for you. If you are the opposite, by contrast, you may thrive in an entrepreneurial environment. There is no right or wrong answer; there is only a right or wrong match to the market needs for that specific role. **In short, if you need to try too hard, it isn't a fit.**

The second bullet point on the prior page should be scrutinized if you find it lurking in a job description. If you hate time constraints and deadlines, you will not add your best value in roles that consistently require you to adhere to them. On the other hand, if you crave deadlines because they inspire your best work, you may be a good fit, as long as you determine that the words are not a proxy for being available 24/7 (if that is not something you are willing and able to do). Be appropriately, but not overly, suspicious of every word.

At times, job descriptions are rather opaque, and sometimes they are quite short. Short descriptions, however, can be very clear if they are written well. For example, consider a role calling for someone with the following qualities:

> *We are looking for someone with high intelligence, who can build rapport, figure things out and get things done. No a**holes.*

Key strengths are needed, and they come through in the short phrases used above: *strategy, intuition, teamwork, negotiation, communication, decisiveness, pragmatism and follow-through.*

More About Job Descriptions

As you are analyzing job descriptions, another way to organize yourself and understand what each role entails is to categorize the component "asks" of the role by the skills, talents and interests they describe.

Note: For the purpose of understanding market needs for one's value proposition, I often advise clients that they do not need to limit their review to open roles in their target geographical area. While there are often some company or regional differences among roles, great insights come from canvassing across roles and regions rather than only reviewing the job descriptions that may be available at a given time in a specific location. For more about market demand for certain skills and talents in certain fields, you can also search online for "top skills" or "top talents" and "[name of your profession]."

Please note that the approach of using job descriptions for your diligence only works so far as there are already jobs available for what you wish to offer to the market. Job descriptions are like training wheels: they will keep you from falling but they can also slow you down. If you need to create a new market or carve out a new role for yourself in order to reach a satisfying match for your priorities and strengths, then you might need to write your own.

I very deliberately wrote the phrase "what you wish to offer to the market" above. Although in this unit we are investigating market needs, it is important that you do not lose sight of the work you have done in prior units and snap back into an impression that the company is in the driver's seat and we all need to conform to its wishes. There are a wide range of organizations and potential roles, and we all make choices about our priorities (or, failing that, make the choice not to actively plan our own careers).

Lastly, on the topic of job descriptions, if you have an annual or periodic review process at your company that is detailed enough to include substantive feedback, consider the needs of the role as expressed in the review as part of your de facto job description. In all cases, take these sources with the proverbial grain of salt and filter them through your personal knowledge. For example, a company may say they want their employees to cultivate certain parts of their roles but incentivize them with compensation and kudos to do otherwise, creating the potential for mismatch and a miscommunication of actual needs.

B. DUE DILIGENCE

There is no end to the ways that you can conduct due diligence on a company, including its own website, press, industry reports, LinkedIn® profiles of its senior management and heads of departments, news articles about and conferences given by such individuals (the latter of which may be memorialized on YouTube, for example), annual reports, slide decks prepared for its client presentations and a host of other materials that come up in internet searches. If you are currently employed with the company and wish to strengthen your value proposition for an internal move or advancement, you may have access to many more resources.

You will also want to conduct due diligence on the type of roles (or clients) you are seeking. One place to start is with thought leaders in the field (industry professionals, investors, donors, recruiters or others): what do they believe is needed to achieve success? Are their general comments applicable to the role, and how can they frame your overall understanding of how a role fits into the larger organizational picture? Can you create an opportunity to connect with and speak directly to these thought leaders – e.g., through informational interviews – if it is appropriate to do so? If not, you can use their guidance as a framework for your conversation with the people with whom you do connect, especially if they are well known and their words carry weight in your field?

> Marc van Zadelhoff, General Manager of IBM Security, for example, wrote that characteristics of a successful cybersecurity professional include **"unbridled curiosity, passion for problem solving, strong ethics, and an understanding of risks**." *See* his article "Cybersecurity Has a Serious Talent Shortage. Here's How to Fix It," in *Harvard Business Review*, May 24, 2017 https://hbr.org/2017/05/cybersecurity-has-a-serious-talent-shortage-heres-how-to-fix-it. If this is your field, his comments may be a place to start.

An important goal with due diligence is to determine your criteria and prioritize information based on what it is important to know about the organization (and its competitors and industry). This information should relate to its overall objectives and how your role would support them. You can then organize it in a way that it is easily read and retrieved. You may, for example, create PDF files or downloads of online information (so your information is not lost if the source is updated or deleted) and links of videos to replay later. You can keep everything in a single folder by company name and any notes or links in a Word or other file, or you can create multiple folders to further categorize information by subject matter.

C. INFORMATIONAL INTERVIEWS

Informational interviews, mentioned above, are a great way to gain an understanding of the needs of a company or across a particular field or industry. For the purpose of establishing your value proposition, you should ask questions that will help you ascertain market needs in relevant roles for someone with the strengths and whether those roles will, in turn, meet your needs. **Make sure, as you choose your informational interview targets, that you find the right people to interview, i.e., people who have enough insight to understand what is needed <u>and</u> are willing and able to share that information in a helpful way.**

People I want to contact for informational interviews:

How I know these are the right people with whom to connect:

Questions I want to ask in informational interviews (use additional pages as needed):

Note: Use a spreadsheet or other means to keep track of your contacts, connectors, stages of interviews, information gathered and next steps (if any). I have samples at www.annemariesegal.com/pipeline.

If you are not on the job hunt but rather are reading this book to move up (or laterally) within your current firm, you may nonetheless wish to informally gather information from others in your industry through informational interviews. You may also wish to schedule time with receptive individuals who are senior, lateral or (in some cases) junior to you, if they are the right people to fill you in about information that will be helpful for you to understand your firm's needs. Don't forget to return the favor!

Akin to informational interviews are conversations with recruiters, who are often great resources, if you take the time to get to know them personally.

If you are having trouble locating the right individuals with whom to connect, first survey your network. Are there people within your network who can make the right connections and are discreet and motivated to help you? Make sure to be very clear that you are asking for information, not looking for a job. (If a job match happens to emerge, and the person with whom you are speaking wishes to recommend you, that's wonderful. But bait and switch – asking for an informational interview and then expecting more – will burn through your network very quickly and put you in a bad light for future requests.)

D. PERSONAL KNOWLEDGE

To reiterate, your personal knowledge of how a company or industry works is not something that you should apply only as a first or last step. Let your growing intuition help you filter the information you receive throughout the process. For example, if you have a personal interest in a certain area and follow news on it regularly, you may have a better sense of the industry than either the press or some of your interview contacts. Use your intuition to verify information if you receive conflicting advice or have a reason to doubt what you are told by any particular source.

I have clients who apply and interview for roles at a whole range of companies – including some that many people would consider dream employers – from the National Hockey League to Marvel Entertainment LLC (and I am sure I do not need to recite for you what either of them do!) as well as clients in hedge funds, healthcare and other fields. Some of them already have a very good sense of the market and find that these strategies only hone their antennae. Others need to get closer to the pulse of an industry and understand what companies are looking for in various candidates, and they find that one or more of these strategies is the best means of doing so.

My personal knowledge about my target industries, companies and roles:

E. WORKSHEETS

As you flip to the worksheets starting on the following page, you will see that I have suggested making additional notes outside of this workbook and then transferring the relevant information here. In particular, I suggest that you "debrief" yourself after an informational interview, writing down anything you learned, before filtering out market needs. This debrief will help the information stay fresh in your mind and also help you record thoughts that may not be specific to market needs but nonetheless may be useful in a future job search or otherwise. There are a sample interview debrief form and additional copies of the following worksheets on my website at www.annemariesegal.com/worksheets.

MARKET NEEDS

Current Role

After making a series of notes, here is the summary of what I have learned about market needs for my current role through the following sources:

A. Job Descriptions

_____

_____

_____

_____

_____

B. Due Diligence

_____

_____

_____

_____

_____

C. Informational Interviews

_____

_____

_____

_____

_____

Market Needs, Page 2: Current Role

D. <u>Personal Knowledge</u>

_____

_____

_____

_____

_____

What information gaps, if any, I must fill:

_____

_____

_____

_____

Additional notes:

_____

_____

_____

_____

_____

MARKET NEEDS

Target Role #1: _____

After making a series of notes, here is the summary of what I have learned about market needs for my first target role (job search or advancement) through the following sources:

A. Job Descriptions

_____

_____

_____

_____

_____

B. Due Diligence

_____

_____

_____

_____

_____

C. Informational Interviews

_____

_____

_____

_____

_____

Market Needs, Page 2: Target Role #1

D. <u>Personal Knowledge</u>

_____

_____

_____

_____

_____

What information gaps, if any, I must fill:

_____

_____

_____

_____

Additional notes:

_____

_____

_____

_____

_____

MARKET NEEDS

Target Role #2: _____

After making a series of notes, here is the summary of what I have learned about market needs for my second target role (job search or advancement) through the following sources:

A. <u>Job Descriptions</u>

_____

_____

_____

_____

_____

B. <u>Due Diligence</u>

_____

_____

_____

_____

_____

C. <u>Informational Interviews</u>

_____

_____

_____

_____

_____

_____

Market Needs, Page 2: Target Role #2

D. <u>Personal Knowledge</u>

_____

_____

_____

_____

_____

What information gaps, if any, I must fill:

_____

_____

_____

_____

Additional notes:

_____

_____

_____

_____

Record any themes you have uncovered about market needs for your strengths:

My Target Market(s):

Challenges My Target Market(s) Are Facing:

How My Strengths Make Me a Fit to Solve Those Challenges:

PART 3:

CREATING A MATCH

UNIT 7 - YOUR VALUE PROPOSITION

Are you ready to create your personal value proposition?

Like those who are hailed as overnight successes – many of whom actually toiled for years outside of the limelight before they were given their due – you can now "without much effort" assemble the key points of your value proposition by taking your results from prior units and synthesizing them here. In summary, the basic premise behind a personal value proposition is:

- *Determine your strengths*

- *Find roles that require those strengths (and meet your needs)*

- *Connect the dots for your audience, i.e., tie your strengths to the call of those roles*

- *Create a case for the benefits you can bring to the organization*

The benefits you can bring to an organization, reflected in the last bullet point, are the ways in which you might solve challenges facing the organization or support its goals.

If you are focused on growth, how can you help the company grow? Do you have examples of how you have managed growth that are beneficial to this new organization (or your current employer, if you are advancing internally), and how can you best access them to explain what value you offer? If you are focused on risk management, what examples do you have of times that you have managed risk, and are these in line with strategies that would be useful for your target? In each case, make sure that your examples reflect not only work that you have done in the past but also what you are interested in continuing to do in the future. Your due diligence in the prior unit will help you uncover an organization's challenges and goals, which are analogous to its needs.

If you have little work experience (in general or related to your new target areas), you will need to persuade your audience of your aptitude rather than rely on examples of benefits that you have brought to other organizations in the past. In that case, I would brainstorm as many examples as possible in which you have demonstrated such aptitude and then vet them for the best fit, related to the type of work you will be doing in the target role.

Personal Value Charts

I have endeavored to make this workbook comprehensive but not voluminous, so I have included three sets of charts to compare your strengths to market needs. My initial suggestion (with an alternative below) is that you summarize the epitome of both your strengths and market needs in the first chart, without gaming it to make a better match on either end. Then read my comments following this first set of charts to see what else you can draw out as helpful additions.

Once you have had a chance to review the match, you can revise as appropriate – reprioritizing or adding additional strengths to round yourself out, or matching yourself to a more suitable market – in the second and third set. There is also a space on the top of each market needs chart (second in each set) to label it based on the specific market or role.

You can find additional copies of the charts on the following pages by visiting my website at annemariesegal.com/worksheets, or you can create your own.

Chicken and Egg Problem

As you preview the following charts, you may be wondering which angle should drive the personal value proposition analysis. Which comes first? Strengths or market needs? It is a great question, and the answer (like many things in life) is that it depends.

If at this stage in your career you are seeking to align your work more closely to who you are and what you value, start with your strengths. This will allow you to explore how well a role will meet your interests, work style, values and preferences while giving you opportunities to use your talents and skills (or develop new ones that would fit how you wish your career to evolve). With this first approach, you will list your top strengths and compare current or target roles to those strengths.

On the other hand, you could be trying to raise your "stock" in the market. For example, you may wish to find stronger ways to appeal to management within your current firm to show you are a compelling candidate to promote or are ready to take on more challenging assignments. You may be seeking to generate a stronger base of clients in an existing business or selling yourself in job interviews. If this is the current posture of your career, start with market needs and use this lens to choose the strengths that best support those needs. With this second approach, you will list market needs and then canvass your strengths to meet those needs. You can also identify gaps in your value proposition that need further support, find ways to get that support and communicate how your other skills, talents and interests will bridge any gaps.

There is the hybrid approach, of course, that I mentioned above. You can create a separate personal value proposition equation from each of the two perspectives and then merge them together. This may be, in fact, how you use the three charts. Even if you do not take the hybrid approach, it behooves you to consider your value proposition from both angles. Regardless of which phase of your career you currently inhabit, as long as you remain employed you should continue to explore your options and sell yourself to the market, so that you continue to be viable, challenged, engaged and appropriately compensated.

Do not reinvent the wheel to complete these charts. Most, if not all, of your answers can be found among your prior responses in this book.

Similar but Distinct Personal Value Propositions

I have worked with clients who hold the role of chief executive, law firm partner, general counsel, trader, government official, media personality, scientist, marketer, project manager, non-profit director, minister, chef and a range of other professional titles. Each of these career choices has a distinct set of parameters but nonetheless wide range of possible market needs that support one's individual skills, talents and priorities.

For example, consider a chief financial officer (let's call her Teresa) who faces a dilemma. She may work at a community bank and hold family life, integrity and service as some of her strongest values. She may also relish the challenges of facilitating corporate strategy, interacting with the board of directors and managing a team of senior executives. Teresa could, in other words, create a compelling case to fill the chief executive role within the bank upon the impending departure of the current CEO.

At the same time, Teresa may be very interested in the arts and considering a move, also in the CEO capacity, to a non-profit organization that supports theater and dance. She could use the value proposition charts in this unit to help her determine which of these roles are better aligned with her strengths and priorities. At the end of the day, Teresa may decide that although the non-profit supports her arts interest, there would be a strong fundraising component and she is not interested in using her talents or leveraging her network in this way. Alternatively, Teresa may find that the organization's fundraising needs offer an opportunity to galvanize her strongest allies in support of a cause with which she truly connects, including some individuals whom she could recruit as new board members of the organization. It could also give her an opportunity to work within a smaller organization, with less regulatory pressure and greater opportunities for hands-on contributions.

On the other hand, Teresa could be in an entirely different situation. She could have been one of a short list of candidates who were considered for the CEO role at her community bank employer and not been chosen. Although she may still have support from the board to continue in her current role, she could also feel some pressure to move on within the next few months and let the new CEO assemble his own team. At this juncture, Teresa may be looking to create a strong value proposition to entice targets she finds compelling to hire her away, either as a CFO or CEO. She would then use the value proposition chart to help her frame the needs of those targets and how they match with her strengths (i.e., the second approach described above).

Tying Benefits You Bring to Your Value Proposition

To understand the benefits that you can bring to an organization, you first need to know its specific goals and challenges. Second, you need to consider how the role that you may hold can help meet each of those needs.

For example, a college intern (let's call him Eric) at a marketing company may find that he has a unique perspective, as all of the other staff members are over 40 years old. Eric understands the mind of today's 20-year-old better than anyone born in the 1960s, 70s, 80s or 90s ever will. He also has a keen eye for color, knows how to tell a compelling story and is an excellent proofreader. Each of these strengths and more – the first of which is literally by accident of his year of birth – may be exactly what the company needs.

At another firm, however, they could already have these needs filled by current staff and instead seek an intern who can take good notes in creative meetings, turn those notes into copy, proofread flawlessly and work long hours into the night to meet project deadlines.

Although Eric is the same person who would be applying to these two roles, he will face very different market needs, and be able to bring (if he also possesses the latter set of strengths) an entirely different set of benefits to the second firm.

Accomplishments

In the accomplishments chart, your goal is to have examples that support your ability to bring benefits to the firm that you have determined (through your due diligence) meet it needs. Please make sure that your examples are sufficiently: (1) universal to appeal to the various audiences you expect to pitch, (2) specific that they tell a story, (3) related to the target role and (4) versatile enough that they could be used to support various questions you may be asked in relation to your value proposition. For example, Eric (above) could be asked about a time he faced two competing deadlines and how he resolved it (a question that goes to both work ethic and judgment). As it is helpful to have a structure for your notes, you can write them in terms of challenges faced, actions taken and results achieved.

For example, if you want to show that you are collaborative, discuss a situation in which a partnership led to a greater benefit than each of you could have achieved individually. Make sure that example has a good story behind it – related to skills you would use in the role – and that you achieved a favorable result (or at least learned a valuable lesson that was a favorable result of sorts for your own career and demonstrates a tangible success for the collaboration, if not the project). It may take some digging and even calling up old colleagues to verify and give more color to the right examples, but it is worth the effort.

Notes I wish to have in hand before completing the charts:

<u>**TAKE 1:**</u>
My Top and Complementary Strengths + My Edge (see p. 66)

Top Strengths:

Complementary Strengths and Edge:

Interests/Values/Preferences:

TAKE 1:

Market Needs (answer per role or across a group of similar roles)

Top Strengths Sought:

Top Needs for the Role(s) (ideas to be generated, problems to be solved, connections to be made, risks to be managed, etc.):

What Else is Needed Be Successful in the Role(s):

Benefits I Can Bring to My Target Organization(s): Take 1

Benefit #1:

Benefit #2:

Benefit #3:

Benefit #4:

Accomplishments that Demonstrate the Benefits I Can Bring

Accomplishment #1:

Accomplishment #2:

Accomplishment #3:

Accomplishment #4:

Now that you have completed the first set, rate the strength of your match. Are your strengths well aligned with market needs, or do you need to readjust one or the other? If the latter, can you call upon additional strengths without losing authenticity or find another role that is more suitable to your value? Please complete the exercises below and try another set.

Where my strengths and market needs are best aligned:

Where the gaps (if any) lie:

My strategy to close the gaps:

Other strengths I can emphasize that are more aligned to the market needs for these role(s):

Other roles that are more aligned to my strengths:

TAKE 2:
My Top and Complementary Strengths + My Edge

Top Strengths:

Complementary Strengths and Edge:

Interests/Values/Preferences:

<u>TAKE 2:</u>

Market Needs (answer per role or across a group of similar roles)

Top Strengths Sought:

Top Needs for the Role(s) (ideas to be generated, problems to be solved, connections to be made, risks to be managed, etc.):

What Else is Needed Be Successful in the Role(s):

Benefits I Can Bring to My Target Organization(s): Take 2

Benefit #1:

Benefit #2:

Benefit #3:

Benefit #4:

Accomplishments that Demonstrate the Benefits I Can Bring

Accomplishment #1:

Accomplishment #2:

Accomplishment #3:

Accomplishment #4:

For your second set, you can again rate the strength of your match. Were you closer this time? Does your list of strengths authentically reflect strong skills and talents you hold? Are you accurately perceiving market needs, or does that need to be tweaked again as well? Does the match feel like a strong, solid pair of strengths and needs?

Where my strengths, my priorities and market needs are best aligned:

Where the gaps (if any) lie:

My strategy to close the gaps:

Other strengths I can emphasize that are more aligned to the market needs for these role(s):

Other roles that are more aligned to my strengths and priorities:

TAKE 3:
My Top and Complementary Strengths + My Edge

Top Strengths:

Complementary Strengths and Edge:

Interests/Values/Preferences:

<u>TAKE 3:</u>

Market Needs (answer per role or across a group of similar roles)

Top Strengths Sought:

Top Needs for the Role(s) (ideas to be generated, problems to be solved, connections to be made, risks to be managed, etc.):

What Else is Needed Be Successful in the Role(s):

Benefits I Can Bring to My Target Organization(s): Take 3

Benefit #1:

Benefit #2:

Benefit #3:

Benefit #4:

Accomplishments that Demonstrate the Benefits I Can Bring

Accomplishment #1:

Accomplishment #2:

Accomplishment #3:

Accomplishment #4:

For this third set, rate the match yet again. If you still have not accurately captured an authentic and compelling personal value proposition for your target market, or if you have created a viable match but feel there is still something missing, turn to Unit 8 (Creating Your Own Market).

Where my strengths and market needs are best aligned:

Where the gaps (if any) lie:

My strategy to close the gaps:

Other strengths I can emphasize that are more aligned to the market needs for these role(s):

Other roles that are more aligned to my strengths:

If you have reached this point in the workbook, further congratulations are in order. You now have your personal value proposition defined and refined in light of your target roles.

CONGRATULATIONS!

Before you complete the next, take a day or two (or at least an hour) to let your work on the prior pages sink in. If there are any final notes or adjustments that you want to make, you can record them here or on page 118. Without letting too much time pass, once you have settled on a core value proposition, you may wish to create an abridged version that fits onto one page for easy reference. See the following page to create a summarized four-part chart of your strengths, market needs, benefits you bring and supporting accomplishments.

Those of my strengths and priorities that do <u>not</u> fit into any of my target roles:

_____

_____

_____

How I can keep myself at the top of my game and my strengths sharp (e.g., serve on a corporate or non-profit board, volunteer, pursue leisure activities or launch a side business):

_____

_____

_____

_____

_____

Do I need to consider finding an interim role that will bring me closer to my goals and is a better fit for my strengths and priorities than what I do currently? ___ Yes ___ No

Notes: _____

_____

_____

_____

_____

_____

ONE-PAGE SUMMARY OF MY PERSONAL VALUE PROPOSITION
(to have ready for interviews, client meetings and for Unit 10)

<u>**My Strengths and Priorities:**</u>	<u>**Market Needs:**</u>
<u>**Benefits I Can Bring:**</u>	<u>**Supporting Accomplishments:**</u>

Key Takeaways from Unit 7:

_____

_____

_____

_____

_____

_____

_____

_____

_____

Further Thoughts or Next Steps:

_____

_____

_____

_____

_____

_____

_____

_____

UNIT 8 - CREATING YOUR OWN MARKET

> The best ideas are the honest ones. Ones born out of personal experience.
> Ones that originated to help a few and ended up helping many.
> - *Simon Sinek*, author of *Find Your Why*

In Unit 6, we discussed market needs, and in Unit 7 we matched your skills, talents and priorities to those needs (based on roles that exist and for which you are currently qualified.) But what if you have not reached a satisfying and feasible match?

What if you still find major gaps – and need to create a bridge – between your strengths and market needs? Or you want or need to create a new market altogether?

I have created my personal value proposition in Unit 7 and can now clearly see a career path that fits my strengths and priorities and existing market needs: ___ Yes ___ No

Note: If you answer "yes" above and wish to create your personal brand and elevator pitch based on your answers in Unit 7, you can turn directly to Unit 9. Otherwise, continue reading this unit.

If something is missing – and I am already aware of what it is – here are the elements I need to revisit in my personal value proposition equation:

_____

_____

_____

_____

If you need help identifying or refining what is missing, turn back to the answers you recorded in Units 1 through 5. At the time you completed those units, your immediate goal was to get everything on the page. You can review them now to prioritize what you have written and consider how your priorities and strengths may lead you on a new path, if you decide that is an appropriate next step.

Hypothetical: Entrepreneurship

An example of how to incorporate a range of interests into your life may be helpful here.

You may have always wanted to write a novel around the topic of family relationships. You also may want to launch a business selling hand-designed clothes and shoes. And maybe, as a third interest, you would like to learn Italian and travel to Italy for cooking classes.

One woman (let's call her Ariana) told me about similar dreams in a wistful voice – as I casually mentioned over a haircut that I was writing my own book – and our conversation happened to take place just as I was in the midst of planning this chapter.

To her surprise, I asked Ariana straightaway which one she was going to do first. After a few seconds, she said confidently that the most important of her dreams was to launch her own business. So we started talking about what that would entail, and how Ariana could build her market. Her dream (now in the words of a goal) is to sell clothes for tall women and size 10+ women's shoes, and she wants to have her own storefront in Norwalk, Connecticut. We talked about how an online business, instead of or in addition to the storefront, might be a good idea to broaden her customer base. It also might be a way to get her started and minimize start-up risks.

There are many aspects that Ariana will need to master to launch and run her business - from suppliers to legal to financing – in addition to refining her offering and finding customers. Yet if she is committed to it, gets the right advice to set herself up well <u>and</u> maintains her primary income stream (or accumulates sufficient savings) to support her in the early years, she can make it happen. The question, like always, is whether she has the requisite *strengths* to do that and whether it aligns with her *priorities.*

At the same time, once Ariana commits to the dress and/or shoe business launch, writing a book and learning Italian are no longer just dreams either. If she becomes comfortable taking appropriate risks, these take the back seat as lesser priorities, but they are elevated from dreams to long-term goals.

Further, Ariana may be able to work these secondary goals into her primary goal. For example, she could write a novel in which the main character needs to manage family relations while launching a business, with some real-life examples (or, in another context, as an outlet and counterpoint to the stresses she encounters as she does so). At the same time, she could arrange to travel to Italy once or twice a year for business, making contacts in the fashion world and taking a weekend cooking class at the tail end of each trip. She could also include Italian words, designs, colors and themes into her sketches, samples and ultimate creations of clothing and shoes.

The keys to making all of these dreams, priorities and goals work together are two-fold. First, Ariana needs to manage her time and energy levels so that she is doing each thing in the order that best propels her goals forward - and keeps her cash flow going through the launch. Second, she needs to maintain the flexibility to tailor [pun intended], adapt and reprioritize different aspects of her goals as needed.

If we did a gap analysis for Ariana, we would tally all of the major areas that she would need to master and determine which were her strengths and which she could learn. Since she will effectively be the CEO of her business – whether or not she has thought of it that way - she will need a much broader skill set than someone who is an employee of another company, as she is now.

For certain of her new role's needs, Ariana may be able to outsource where she doesn't have the skills (such as website design, payroll and other aspects that go into running a business), but she will need to understand the component parts that she is outsourcing in order to stay on top of her consultants and contractors. She can do this by taking classes, getting advice from another business owner or hiring someone to coach her through the process. In other areas (such as building credibility with customers, or creating the vision for the products she will sell), if Ariana does not have the requisite talents and skills at the time of launch or shortly thereafter, her business is unlikely to be a success. Further aspects of her new CEO/Designer role – such as how to lead and manage a growing team effectively – cannot be effectively outsourced, but they can be learned over time.

My initial impression of this hypothetical, as it could apply to my own situation, is:

_____

_____

_____

_____

If reading the above hypothetical rekindles any dreams of becoming an entrepreneur, here are some first steps I can take – and people who can help me – to explore and vet my ideas:

_____

_____

_____

_____

New Markets All Around You

We all have the opportunity every day to create a new market for our strengths – and create a big idea (or more than one) – if we only are open to problems that need solving and we are uniquely situated to solve. Rather than try to generate ideas in isolation, we need to get out of our comfort zones, talk to people and figure out what is needed.

Take the real-life case of Rich Mason, a Maryland biologist who invented and is marketing a device that rescues wildlife, after hearing from friends and others about frogs, mice and chipmunks and other small animals falling into and drowning in pools. He created the invention in his garage in 2005, using some scrap foam and a sewing machine, and now sells it through Walmart, Amazon and other outlets, with a recommendation from the U.S. Humane Society among other organizations. (See www.froglog.us.)

Inventions can be products or services, and they can be entirely new or simply a process improvement that drives growth or cuts expenses. In other words, you can either serve an existing market with an incremental improvement or have a bold, innovative value proposition that you use to create a new market.

How I can keep my "ear to the ground" regarding professional and personal interests that might lead to a new market:

Who can help me in these efforts (people I already know and can meet):

Problems that I already know need solving (and I am uniquely positioned to solve):

Hypotheticals: Changing Fields

Although entrepreneurship is often at the heart of creating a new market, sometimes a change of fields (to a new type of role within an established company) is a better fit. To understand what appeals to you most – in response your overall gut feeling that you need a career change – you may need to break down your interests, values and preferences into the relevant aspects of each potential target role.

For example, maybe you always wanted to be a doctor, but you were not sure you had "what it takes" to make it through medical school. Instead, you may have gone into a completely unrelated field, such as accounting. Even if it is too late at this point in your career to become a doctor, you could go back to school and become a nurse. (My stepfather did this in his 50s actually, with the support of my mother who was able to help him manifest a version of this dream in a new way. He was a nurse for 10 years before retiring from his second career, and in many ways he was a pioneer in his new field, both as a second-careerist and as one of the few male nurses on staff at that time.)

On the other hand, maybe the reason you decided not to go to medical school is because you realized you did not want to be around all that blood, so working as a nurse is not a fit either. You may have considered veterinary school, because you are a big animal lover, but decided to exclude it for the same reasons. Yet now, you are in a desk job and very unhappy. You like the patient–oriented aspect of the medical field, and you feel that you do not have a real connection with people who share your same interests and values. In this case, should you try to make a go of something else in medicine, and what options would be available?

In career-change scenarios, informational interviewing becomes invaluable. You can explore what it would be like to be in a job on a day-to-day basis, and you can draw on the resources of your extended network for the exploration and vetting of ideas. Talk to a wide range of people doing what you think you might like to do. Are they happy with their choices? Do they have personalities, values, interests, skills, talents and goals similar to you?

As we explore further, sometimes we find that our interests have transformed over the years. What may have started as an interest in medicine could have turned into an interest in veterinary medicine, and may have further become an interest in animals more generally. Once you understand the progression and current iteration of your interests, you are in a better position to know how to incorporate them into your life. There are a wide variety of ways to satisfy an interest in animals, from designing cute animal T-shirts, magnets and mugs to sell on Etsy.com to working at a local farm on the weekends, and from volunteering at a non-profit organization that rescues abandoned animals to sitting on the board of directors of an aquarium or natural history museum. Or, of course, you could decide to return to an earlier role you had considered and train to become a veterinarian.

As another example of a career transition, I have an attorney client (let's call him Ryan) who has been practicing for years within a very niche area. Ryan was offered an in-house position that would require him to exhibit a much broader set of skills and substantive knowledge than he currently possesses. He was nervous about getting up to speed and wondered if it was the right role for him. In addition, he had a nagging concern of being called out as a fraud once the firm realized how narrow his practice had been to date.

Ryan and I talked about his long-term goals and whether he wanted (i.e., had the *interest*) to stay within his niche or branch out. He said he was very interested in expanding his substantive knowledge and even was contemplating a move to the business side. We then discussed his skills and talents, including the strong instincts he has demonstrated on a range of legal issues, which indicate he has the judgment and issue-spotting capabilities to break into new areas of law (at least at the level initially expected in the role, if not yet as an expert) in a relatively short period of time. Ryan's decision about the potential transition was made easier by viewing it not as an overwhelming, untenable prospect but a logical (and heartfelt) analysis of his priorities, talents and skills.

My initial impressions of these hypotheticals, as they could apply to my own situation, are:

_____

_____

If I can see aspects of myself in the above hypotheticals, here are some first steps I can take – and people who can help me – to explore and vet my ideas:

_____

_____

_____

Recovering from Career Inertia

As a career coach, I meet with clients all the time who feel boxed into the current iteration of their profession and cannot get out.

As another example, imagine a lawyer (let's call him Sam) who throughout law school was enthralled with the idea of working as an attorney in the publishing industry. Instead, he found himself litigating in a practice area with which he felt no affinity and constantly faced ethical challenges, unable to find a role in publishing because the market was in a downturn when he first got out of law school and did not improve in the years directly thereafter. He had no chance to make the switch to his dream job, in other words, because he needed to focus on making his billable hour requirements and keeping his bosses and clients happy.

Ten years have passed. Now he hates his law practice, and that animosity is spilling over into the rest of his life. He is concerned (and has received feedback) that he is too senior for people to take a chance on him in a new industry and he doesn't know how to break in anyway, even if he could. In short, he may have missed the window of opportunity on this particular dream job. Yet the idea of generating an entirely new market for himself sounds daunting and more energy than he can muster, and he has no other ideas.

There are a million reasons why we lose touch with our dream jobs, and the million-dollar question is always what we should do next. Fortunately for you, if you have had the perseverance to get this far in the book, you probably have the perseverance to make a meaningful transition in your life. Take a look at what you have listed as your interests, skills and talents. Is the dream job of old still the dream job of today?

If I need of a career transition and have a dream job in mind, here's what it is:

_____

_____

_____

This job would change my life because I would be able to:

_____

_____

If you are still unsure about whether making your dream job a reality will actually bring you satisfaction in your career, the next step is to line up informational interviews with people who are actually doing what you think you want to do next. You can meet them if you set your mind to it. Often people are more than willing to share about their careers if you are genuinely interested, respectful and willing to listen.

At this early stage, you are not trying to sell yourself. You are on a reconnaissance mission. You need to assess the gap and decide what effort will be required to fill it, plus the likelihood of success. If you do not have the skills, do you have the talent to acquire them? Are you willing to make the commitment? Can you find others who have made a similar transition, and what did they need to make it effectively? And, key question: would you actually enjoy what you would be doing on a daily basis?

Who can give me more information about my dream job, including how it would be to work in that job on a daily basis:

_____

_____

_____

Who has made a similar transition and can help me understand market needs and what I would need to build my personal value proposition:

_____

_____

_____

Questions I can ask them:

_____

_____

_____

At the same time, take a look at your alternatives. If we return to be example of Sam, the attorney who wanted to be in the publishing industry early in his career and now hopes to make the change, why was he interested in publishing? Maybe he always wanted to be an author but did not think he had the talent, so he wanted a chance to work with top authors and be engaged in writing that way. Now, years later, he has a second chance to reconsider his first career choice. If, in retrospect, being a writer is now a better (and more feasible) choice than being involved in an industry that supports writers, Sam could be wasting valuable time if he focuses on creating a transition to publishing law.

As Sam is contemplating his options, he also may be able to shift some elements of his "daily grind" away from his current practice area and into something he finds more fulfilling that would also give him the freedom to try his hand at the writing. If he wants to be involved in a community of writers in order to keep himself on track and motivated, he can take a writing class, or he can join or create his own writing group that meets periodically (in person or virtually) and reviews each other's work. He can also start a blog or submit to publications to get feedback on his writing, all while maintaining his current role as an attorney. These activities would take time and involve some risk that they may not pan out, but if Sam is committed the investments of time and risk are worth it (especially considering the alternative, which is remaining stuck in an unfulfilling career).

Other ideas for Sam to bridge to his writing interests and experiment with how to incorporate them into his law practice include representing a few authors *pro bono* on publishing contracts to get experience in and enjoyment out of the field, teaching legal writing at his firm, mentoring young students who want to become better writers, writing book reviews (for legal, fiction or other books) or organizing and hosting events that bring famous writers to town. Again, all of these can be done to help get him closer to his evolving vision for his dream job and make the current one more bearable.

What I can do that could be a bridge to my dream job and/or create alternatives for me:

_____

_____

_____

_____

_____

Experiments and Experience

In some ways, we are at a pivotal point in history. Many more opportunities are available to us than in years past, as the internet has allowed us to create micro-communities of interests spread across many miles of physical territory. You can look at your own situation and determine the type of market(s) you would like to explore or build for yourself. Get out and talk with people, experiment, experience, volunteer, create a side business, take a course and/or find other ways to learn and grow. Not only will you get more meaning out of your professional life, but also you will be growing your value proposition in line with your strengths and priorities.

Interests I have thought about turning into a side venture or new career:

What intrigues me about the possibilities:

What else I need to know:

Concrete steps I can take in the right direction:

If I need more courage, how I can find the courage:

If I need more skills, how I can get the skills:

What I would be doing on a daily basis in my new role:

How my life and career might change for the better:

What I would need to adjust or leave behind:

What else I should be considering (including financial, health and other factors):

How I can address those considerations:

Whom I would need to bring on board for the change, and how I can present it to them:

What risks I would face:

How prepared I feel to take those risks:

How I could remove other "blocks" that may stall/inhibit me from achieving this change:

Additional notes:

PART 4:

COMMUNICATING YOUR VALUE

UNIT 9 - YOUR PERSONAL BRAND

With your personal value proposition now established, we will outline a thematic approach to personal branding, which you can expand in further detail and apply to the many aspects of branding in your professional life.

In some ways, branding is simply an extension of the long-standing concept of reputation, although reputation management has evolved in the digital age. In an interconnected world, in which people across the globe can meet just about any of us online before being introduced in person, we each have the opportunity (and, if we maintain a digital presence that we want to reflect on us favorably, the responsibility) to thoughtfully craft and propel a message that is accessible 24/7 worldwide. So branding becomes every communication with an audience, as I outline further on the following pages.

That said, the best branding is not only compelling, it is also authentic, tying together our online and offline selves. If you get your personal value proposition right, you can build your personal branding on that solid base. It will be not a mask or a costume that you pull out on special occasions but rather an exercise in being true to yourself. While you may not always feel inspired to "live up to" what you have determined you can offer through your value proposition – we all can feel stuck, tired, distracted or overwhelmed and may need to stretch ourselves from time to time – if your brand truly fits, it will adapt to your best, worst and all other days.

Achieving Authenticity in Branding

I remember hosting a networking event a few years ago, and one of the women who attended (let's call her Kate) asked me for my thoughts on branding. Kate told me she was a partner in a Big 4 accounting firm and maintained a conservative image she felt was in keeping with her role as a risk manager for her clients. Kate further shared that she wanted to become more proactive in creating her brand, but she was afraid she didn't have enough energy to do that. She then added that when she had conveyed this same thought to her mentor the prior week, he advised her that if it took a lot of energy to maintain her brand, it probably wasn't the right brand. I wholeheartedly agree.

In fact, Kate has the opportunity to create a brand that works for her and her market. What are some of the reasons Kate may feel personal branding requires more time and energy than she is willing to invest? Maybe she has a false sense of what branding means. Perhaps she does not have enough self-awareness to know which image she wishes to project. Alternatively, she could perceive a tacit "branding standard" in her industry that she feels she needs to meet 100% of the time, whether or not it is actually helpful to her career trajectory and sense of self or necessary to project a fitting professional image to her clients.

For example, if Kate thinks that getting branding right means she should wake up at 4:00 am every morning to perfect and color-coordinate her hair, face, nails, outfit and accessories, she may soon run out of steam. This type of attention to her brand only makes sense if Kate feels energized by doing these things rather than obligated to do them. A panelist at a highly-publicized personal branding seminar I once attended gushed brightly that she does just that: wake up very early to maintain her highly polished, no-hair-out-of-place brand, then hop on a train to the city to arrive before the masses descend. Yet the panelist sounded excited when she discussed her routine and subsequent tucked, tied and manicured day, unlike many of us in the audience (this author included) who were overwhelmed just hearing her tell it.

Having a personal brand does not mean we constantly strive to meet someone else's (or even our own) idea of perfection, unless that is truly what we want to be the essence of our branding. In fact, if we are wound up too tight, we cannot do our best work. Instead, **branding is a form of communication. Who are we? What do we want the world to know about us? How can we best tell others about ourselves in a positive way?**

Yes, we are presenting our best selves, but we choose what that means. If we feel the best manifestation of ourselves is a meticulously put-together image – because we gain peace-of-mind and joy from it – then that is an authentic and compelling brand. Otherwise, we may prefer to maintain a minimalist look and grow our brand in other strategic ways, projecting our base of confidence from that. Or a bit of our own flair, if it suits us and our market.

What if Kate believes branding takes too much energy because it means setting a personal standard that requires a consistent, high level of time and attention to meet? That may be true, although being a professional requires us to invest considerable time in any case. We sometimes need to work when we would rather be playing. We may need to be serious when something strikes us as astronomically absurd or project a light-hearted and funny sense of humor when we feel like anything but laughing.

Branding, if authentic, actually lessens our tension about how to present ourselves. We know who we are, and we do not need to doubt our self worth. While we can go "off script" at any time if we feel the need, the more we get in touch with ourselves, the more our brand is not a role to play but rather simply who we are. In Kate's case, I suggested that she find a way to streamline her brand where possible (saving energy and time) while considering how to meet both her own standards and the expectations of her market (if, after full consideration, each of her perceived expectations were valid).

In some corners, the ideas above may sound like a radical way to approach branding, but consider the alternative. Individually and as a society, is it better that we all live our lives based on our perceived (and potentially inaccurate) view of how others believe we *should* be? Imagine a never-ending cycle of "shoulds," with each of us meeting perceived expectations of our intended audiences, and none of us knowing who we actually are or who anyone else really is either, because we are all so busy idealizing ourselves through brand-building.

So if we start from the base of the pyramid – our personal value propositions – we can build our brands organically, rather than haphazardly. We can base them on our own strengths rather than mosaics of various pieces borrowed from others, including the early expectations of our parents, teachers, bosses at our first jobs and all the other input we have received along the way, that have come together as an inconsistent and incomplete projection of who we are today. If we base our brands in our own priorities and strengths, we no longer need to push ourselves to create a personal brand, we can live each day in our own element.

Where Branding Emerges

Every element of communication is an aspect of our personal brand, from the way we walk and speak (or "walk and talk") to the choice of artwork (if any) we hang on our walls. For example, consider these more and less obvious aspects of branding:

Tone of voice
Clothing choice
Word choice and grammar
Body language
Posture and gait

Your inner circle of friends
Peers with whom you regularly interact (online and offline)
Organizations you join and support
Your mentors, sponsors and others who will vouch for you
Your interests and activities
How you prioritize your time

Articles you write
Ideas you share (including in work or client meetings)
Your website and social media presence on various platforms

Resumes
LinkedIn profiles
Emails
Cover letters
Voicemail messages

Email signatures
Voicemail messages
Out of office messages

As I said above, every aspect of your workday – and, in the digital age, many aspects of your personal life – comes together to create your brand.

What I have already aligned to the personal brand I wish to project:

_____

_____

_____

_____

_____

Elements above that I need to revisit, revise or retool to match my brand:

_____

_____

_____

_____

Other branding elements of and ways I can define my brand:

_____

_____

_____

What I want to do first:

_____

_____

How and when I can make changes to my brand:

_____

_____

_____

_____

How I can create opportunities to showcase or become known for my personal brand:

_____

_____

_____

How my brand intersects with the image that my current organization wants to project and/or the image that I believe that I should project for my career/role:

_____

_____

How important it is to me that I align my personal brand to my organization and/or role:

_____

How important it is to my organization that I align my brand to its brand and/or my role:

_____

How Your Brand Works on Your Resume

As I was writing this chapter, I had a call with a law firm partner (let's call her Wendy) who wanted me to revise her resume and cover letter because she was not getting any interviews despite applying to numerous in-house legal and compliance roles. Among the other issues and areas of potential improvement we discussed, I mentioned that the career narrative Wendy presented to me on the phone was not evident on her resume. On the page, she presented as a garden-variety litigator with significant trial experience. This was not a negative, of course, but it lacked depth and the sense of direction Wendy had for her career.

When we spoke, by contrast, Wendy offered that what she brings to the table is her ability to investigate the weak points in a company's risk management regime and understand how people and systems fit together. "It's like a puzzle," she said. "Often I find that my clients can avoid future litigation by addressing recurring problems." She was looking for a role that allowed her to do just that, but she was not connecting the dots for her target audience (future employers) to see that this was a key part of the value she offered as a candidate.

Rolling Your Personal Value Proposition into a Personal Brand

So what is a compelling, consistent and authentic personal brand and how do you achieve it?

Once you understand how your personal value proposition supports your brand, you will find many new opportunities to demonstrate your value by branding. Here are some exercises to facilitate your thinking. Feel free to poll friends and colleagues for more ideas.

Key words or concepts for branding that I can pull from my value proposition:

_____

_____

_____

_____

_____

_____

Others I admire who exhibit one or more of the same strengths:

_____

_____

_____

What they do or say that makes me aware they possess those strengths:

_____

_____

_____

_____

What is most and least effective about how they project their brands:

_____

_____

_____

_____

The direction I wish to take my career:

How I have seen others effectively brand themselves in that same career direction:

If I don't have any examples of effective branding to follow, what I can do to find them:

Remember that what works for one person as a brand may not always work for another. For example, if you are an information technology executive who is always checking his phone in meetings, you may be conveying a personal brand of being responsive and connected. Someone in another field, by contrast, may convey that he is uncaring or uninterested in the conversation or group. Take note of how your brand will be received by your audience.

Also note those elements of your brand that relate specifically to what you offer the market. Whether it is your resume, social media presence or outgoing voicemail message, think thematically about how you can convey your strengths. If you want to convey that you are organized and execution-focused, for example, you can translate that into a brand and communicate it to your audience. Every interaction that you have, document you draft and message you deliver (along with your attire, body language and tone of voice) presents a new opportunity to show your ability to present organized, results-driven solutions. Consider how the themes that are most relevant to your brand in that case would differ from someone whose greatest strengths are risk-taking and creativity.

The thematic approach to branding applies to all aspects of your communications, and you should be cognizant of market needs. For example, although you may see your value as someone who gets "into the weeds" on projects to make sure you understand every single element that needs to be addressed, you may also wish to temper that with executive summaries of your reports so that others on your team – especially those who are not as detail-oriented – can reap the benefit of your labors. The goal in rolling your value proposition into a brand is not to impress others with your strengths but to put yourself into the service of others, so you are known for those strengths and get the call when your strengths are needed.

How I can best communicate my strengths as elements of my brand:

Top Strengths	Personal Branding Narrative/Elements
1.	

2.	

Complementary Strengths	Personal Branding Narrative/Elements
3.	
4.	
5.	

Addressing Negativity About or Perceived Detractions from Your Brand

Let's take another look at the potential for mismatch between your strengths and how these can be conveyed (or contradicted) by the image that you project.

Imagine someone (let's call her Claire) sees herself as having great attention to detail. Her colleagues and clients, by contrast, perceive her someone who slows down projects because she cannot focus on the larger picture of what the organization or client is trying to achieve. Claire wants to change this image, but she does not want to lose the essence of her value proposition: that she can alert her boss and team to the red flags and potential snags that others miss.

This is not only a branding issue; it is a value proposition issue. Claire is misreading her market. While her employer and clients value her issue-spotting, they expect her to prioritize the issues rather than just identifying them. If she recognizes a disconnect between her perception and others', Claire may at an inflection point in her career and grow into both a new value proposition and a new brand.

Another professional (let's call him Jake) may see himself as highly organized while others are distracted by what appears to be disordered piles of papers around his desk. Jake can present himself well in meetings and on calls, but those who pass his office – including the CEO and CFO, who have never heard him speak – may be dissuaded to promote him due to a messy desk.

This is a branding issue. Jake can take a day to create new files for all of these documents, and he may discard or scan some of them for safekeeping. He may need to lobby internally for more storage space, but the investment is worth his time. This is an example of how getting feedback from others is helpful. (Does management see Jake as promotable or not? Is his disorder perceived as a sign of ingenuity or inefficiency?) By knowing and managing his public perception in this one key way, Jake will improve his personal brand and potential for advancement.

As a third example, you may see yourself as a leader but come across to others as being critical or not valuing their ideas. This could be a hybrid issue, both something that you need to rethink from a value proposition perspective and an adjustment you can make to your personal brand. Always ask yourself how certain actions serve you and your market, and you will set yourself on a better path.

We all know when someone else wants to project a personal brand that is incongruous with how they generally act. It fails when they do so; and it will fail if we do so as well.

- Georgia says she's an adept communicator, but when she leaves a voicemail message you can't understand what she is saying.

- Bryce touts himself as having good judgment, but his comments in meetings make it clear he is does not understand the goals of his manager or the group.

- Henry says he is responsive but never gets back to you when you email or call him.

- Isabel says she is a people-person and works well with all levels of employees, but she is consistently rude to the receptionist on the way in the door.

- Kevin calls himself flexible and solution-oriented, but he puts up roadblocks every time an idea is proposed, without offering any viable alternatives.

Attentive branding keeps you honest about your strengths and how you are perceived, and it serves as a check on whether you are branding yourself in an authentic way that is helpful to meet both market needs and your own. Keeping up an authentic brand involves continually evaluating and firming up your strengths while making changes as needed to align your brand to your career *and* align your career to your value proposition (which supports your brand).

What (if anything) I want as part of my brand but have not incorporated into my daily life:

_____

_____

_____

More ways I can align my value proposition and brand:

_____

_____

_____

_____

Further Thoughts on Personal Branding

I hope you can now appreciate how your personal brand has the capacity to be more authentic if it comes from a place of strength and how "brand management" is more effective if it is accompanied by a commitment to be true to yourself. With this base, you can explore branding further and experiment until you find the elements of a personal brand that fit you best.

Personal brands, of course, evolve over time as we change and grow. We can achieve transformation at any point of our lives and create a corresponding adjustment to our brands, being mindful of the messages we are communicating at each stage in the process.

As I often say to clients, you can convey a very focused or versatile brand – or something in between – depending on where you are in your personal growth. Weave together the strands of your own truth as they become available to you. Life is a process of getting to know ourselves and the people, places and things that come across our paths. Our brands, if viewed holistically, evolve along with this process.

UNIT 10 – YOUR ELEVATOR PITCH(ES)

The concept behind an elevator pitch is ridiculously straightforward.

If you have only 30 seconds to two minutes to tell people about yourself, what should they know? Your elevator pitch is the first words out of your mouth after, "Hi, I'm David." (Getting your own name right, one would hope, will not be the challenge.)

Meeting that challenge – what to say next? – is an exercise in knowing your audience and how you can make a meaningful, motivating connection with them, as well as the right tone for the environment in which the meeting is taking place.

In this chapter, we will explore some different avenues to arrive at an elevator pitch. The first key point is that there is no <u>single</u> elevator pitch that works for every situation. Let me put this another way: while you can spend time memorizing the three key things you want to say about yourself, they may not be the most compelling points for every audience.

One point to remember as you craft a few elevator pitches to have at the ready, or create a specific one for an upcoming meeting or event, is to make sure it is consistent with the information your audience may already know about you. For example, what do your LinkedIn profile, website and/or biography on your firm's webpage communicate? What is your audience expecting from prior interactions, if any?

Your elevator pitch does not need to prioritize the same information or sound exactly as you appear online or have come across in prior interactions with the same audience. If all of your presentations are consistent, it will add to your credibility, but you also have the opportunity to curate the message and details you present about yourself in every social interaction. If you find that your elevator pitches are *consistently* diverting from the otherwise available information about you – or your personal value proposition as you summarized on page 115 – it may be time to rebrand such sources or reconsider your pitch.

A. YOUR WRITTEN ELEVATOR PITCHES

Since I have already opened the door to written elevator pitches, let's start there. How can you introduce yourself in writing and meet the competing objectives of being (1) brief and (2) differentiated. To return to our chef example, here are five different written elevator pitches for chefs that speak to each one's skills, talents, values and interests:

I am a chef who is passionate about creating respect for world cultures by engaging children through food.

As a chef and teacher, I help working parents get more value out of their weekly food budget by creating easy, healthy dinners.

As a chef to the stars, I create innovative vegan menus (paired with wine, of course) to satisfy the most discriminating palates.

Toasted as a top chef in New Orleans, I also own three highly successful seafood restaurants in San Francisco, Miami and New York City.

In my 10+ years as a chef, I have run two catering operations and worked both front and back of the house.

Remember, a written elevator pitch is an appetizer, not the main course. Use interesting words – including keywords people might search to find someone like you – to describe yourself. Draw in your audience. Be someone people want to meet, trust, hire and support.

Sometimes a compelling introduction means sharing your values or touting your accomplishments, especially if you wish to demonstrate you are the right fit for a specific audience. At other times, your introduction may be more descriptive, although it does not need to be boring! Further, your calling card may be humor or brevity, especially if you are already a known quantity in the market or your industry. It depends on your personality, goals, brand, seniority, career track, values, risk-tolerance and other factors.

To appreciate the diversity of presentation styles, consider, for example, CEO Richard Branson's very brief description of himself on LinkedIn (current as of this writing), coupled with a cover shot of his book, *Finding My Virginity*:

> *Tie-loathing adventurer and thrill seeker, who believes in turning ideas into reality. Otherwise known as Dr Yes at Virgin!*

Compare the above to the first sentences of each of the first two paragraphs of CEO Andrea Jung's LinkedIn profile (current as of this writing):

> *Andrea Jung is President and Chief Executive Officer of Grameen America, the fastest-growing microfinance organization in the United States.*

> *Ms. Jung, the longest serving female chief executive in the Fortune 500, is respected as a trailblazer for women's empowerment.*

Ms. Jung has cultivated a refined approach that is quite divergent from Mr. Branson's brand, and I note that she presents herself in the third person. Although first person is generally more engaging to the reader, third person can imply a certain gatekeeping and professional grooming that is in keeping with some personal brands.

What I believe is most compelling about me professionally (and, if applicable, personally):

How I believe others currently see me:

The image I wish to convey:

What is online or in print about me already that I can revise:

What is online or in print about me already that I cannot revise:

How the available online and in-print information compares to my current pitch:

Other pitches that could be helpful to review as I write my own:

Phrases I may wish to include in my written elevator pitch:

What I need to resolve (if anything) before committing to a final version:

My first shot at writing the pitch:

What is missing in the above, if anything:

My second shot at writing the pitch:

Additional revisions:

The various platforms on which I may use a written pitch:

Variations I might make to the above for those platforms:

Who should review these pitches before they go live (and why):

B. YOUR SPOKEN ELEVATOR PITCHES

Audience

Unlike your written pitches, which often can be seen by anyone in a variety of contexts and should likely be more universal, you have more flexibility with your spoken elevator pitch (unless you are on camera or otherwise recorded, in which case you may stick to a more universal pitch, unless a specific one is appropriate under the circumstances).

In particular, the adaptations you will want to make to your spoken pitch are audience-driven. Here are some key questions to ask yourself: What are the needs of your audience? What are you offering? How does it benefit them? How much do they need (if at all) what you are offering? What message is likely to trigger a positive response?

Audiences can vary widely. They can be friendly, neutral or even antagonistic. Imagine the latter, for example, if you are put up for a role and have both supporters and detractors. Your pitch needs to consider both audiences, if you want to be successful. In addition, your audience may be one person or an entire room, and your "real" audience may not even be the person with whom you are speaking but one to whom information will be conveyed at a later point. You also may, in a few cases, need to make a "Hail Mary" elevator pitch, knowing you are highly unlikely to be chosen but giving it your best shot. In all of these cases, especially the latter one, you need to choose between sticking to your core message or going out on a limb (and outside of your comfort zone) to make the connection.

Target audiences for my elevator pitches include:

1) _____

_____

2) _____

_____

3) _____

_____

4) _____

_____

5) _____

_____

What I know (from research, personal information, etc.) about these audiences:

1) _____

_____

2) _____

_____

3) _____

_____

4) _____

_____

5) _____

_____

Strengths (and benefits I can bring) that I may want to emphasize for these audiences:

1) _____

_____

2) _____

_____

3) _____

_____

4) _____

_____

5) _____

_____

C. MORE ABOUT ELEVATOR PITCHES

Context

In addition to audience, consideration of the context is critical. What is the premise of your conversation? Are you making the initial connection, or has an introduction been created for you? Have you been invited to "sell" yourself and given any parameters to do that?

The elevator pitch is a dance between you and your audience. If you are lively and engaging, and you have something to offer of value, imagine how your value can serve your audience. **Your pitch then becomes an exercise in facilitating others in the pursuit of their goals, not convincing them that you are worthy of their time, money or attention.**

When You Are Undecided About Your Career Path

I want to make a quick side note here for those who are still undecided about their goals and value propositions. As I have said to clients on many occasions, there is nothing wrong with being undecided. Take pains, however, not to appear confused. Introducing yourself as dual-tracking your options or being open to new opportunities is different than expecting your audience to sort out the future of your professional life. If you need career guidance, seek it from the appropriate channels, not the audiences of your elevator pitch.

How I can appear flexible and open without coming across as confused:

Meeting New People in Interesting Places

Prospective clients are everywhere, but this does not mean that we need to trot out a dog-and-pony show every time we meet someone who could potentially become a client. We can be more strategic than that and avoid wearing ourselves out by chasing every possible lead.

I once gained a new client, for example, at a summer cocktail party that was held on the expansive balcony of a tall and impressive building in New York City. I am certain it was because I introduced myself not as an executive coach but with a lighter touch. When asked, "So what do you do?" I raised my glass slightly and answered, simply and confidently, "I help change lives." Intrigued, he asked more questions, and I explained further. Then my new friend (and future client) gushed, "I clearly need your help. Can you give me your card?" I had struck a chord by listening and following my intuition about how to present myself.

Although I wasn't gunning for business that evening – it was an event in honor of a friend's many accomplishments, and I was there to support her – there was no reason not to make professional connections at the same time (as long as I enjoyed the refreshing value of a social evening by not "working" the event).

I tell this story because often that lighter, direct touch is exactly what we need, using words that speak to people rather than job titles. A dentist might say, smiling bright, "Well, I am the one that tells people to floss." A health care marketer could offer, "I help hospitals tell their stories, which isn't always an easy thing." The air of mystery, and the act of letting others draw out your story as you drop strategic hints – if you make sure they are relatively obvious ones – can make for more interesting conversations. When everyone is in a friendly mood, you can otherwise come across as stiff, pushy or conceited. (In Mr. Branson's LinkedIn profile, you almost get the sense that his life is one big cocktail party – his profile included – and you can guess it is intentional and aligns with his personal brand.)

I also tell this story to drive home the point that, in addition to the hours some of us spend researching the market, getting to know targets and coming up with the best string of words that we can call up to highlight certain points about ourselves, we need to remember that we are speaking to a specific someone *in the moment*.

People don't like to be pitched, especially at parties. They like to interact in a conversation that unfolds naturally and seemingly effortlessly, rather than having to hear yet another individual try to sell them something when they should be having some well-deserved fun and relaxation. If you want to know the best elevator pitch in that context, ask yourself, "what does the moment call for in the space between us, as two individuals who are communicating with each other at this particular point in time?"

In summary:

- become knowledgeable about your audience's needs,
- know yourself and your value, including how you can benefit your audience,
- watch for cues in the moment, and
- never lose sight of the spark.

A Tale of Two Interests

Sometimes interests that seem completely unrelated to one's career, in the right context, can be game-changers. For example, imagine someone (let's call him Peter) who – in addition to being a highly respected chef – is an avid surfer.

In Peter's case, he can easily weave his surfing interest into his personal value proposition, brand and elevator pitch or use it to connect with potential clients, investors or employers. In fact, he may be losing opportunities to grow his career and align it with his interests if he limits his conversation to purely "professional" aspects.

Now imagine you are at a cocktail party with Peter:

"Hey Peter, tell me about yourself."

"I'm a chef and a surfer…."

What is your reaction?

Peter has just added a potentially compelling new element to the conversation. If you are only interested in talking about his cooking, recipes, favorite restaurants and the like, you can certainly pursue that line of conversation (in that case, your next line might be "Wow, that's cool. What do you like to cook?"). But if you happen to also enjoy surfing, have done it once or twice or wish you could learn to surf one day, you may be intrigued to ask more.

Peter may further share that his interest in surfing has influenced his style of cooking, if he thinks his audience is open to more. (Always watch the body language and eye contact of your audience.) He could mention in a humorous way that he has come to the realization, after many years of wishing otherwise, that food is not only about the taste. The cardiovascular demands of surfing necessitate a nourishing, high-protein diet.

If you remain engaged, Peter may turn the conversation up a notch and talk about how avocados are a source of healthy fat or describe how most restaurants focus not on health but only on providing "tasty" meals that could be far from what we would want to eat if we knew what was in them. He has created a basis to explain his food philosophy without sounding like he is preaching – assuming, that is, that he doesn't actually preach – and he certainly will be remembered long after the cocktail party is over.

Peter's unrelated interest – surfing – has created an opening for a greater and more authentic connection with you and other sympathetic partygoers than might have been possible if these two elements (cooking and surfing) had not been introduced together. The conversation can cut through layers and layers of ever-evolving small talk if the "match" is a valuable one and both speakers are on the same page.

If there is no match – i.e., you or the other person involved in the conversation with Peter has no interest in either surfing or healthy eating – then Peter may have "lost" the chance to connect, but it is likely that there was no affinity in that case. One day, Peter just may connect with someone who is very keen on his approach to cooking and wants to help him launch a restaurant or hire him as a personal chef. Note in this example, of course, that I am assuming surfing *actually* is key to Peter and has influenced his way of life. Professing interests as ruses for the sake of conversation starters will not lead you to those with whom you have the best chance of connection. If it is not authentic, you will not be compelling.

I used surfing as an entry point here, and you may imagine a diverse range of professions for which it might be a great counterpoint or involve a complementary set of skills. A number of venture capitalists, for example, have compared the strategy, positioning and patience needed for surfing as similar to that needed for investing (a cross-training of talents as I mentioned in Unit 5). Other interests can provide similar crossovers, as long as you know both yourself and your audience, which is our work here in this book.

When Your Elevator Pitch Sounds Like Everyone Else's

If you are reading the above, you may say, "Great, I'm not like Peter. What I do is not very interesting, and I have no idea how to turn it into a compelling elevator pitch." Wow, give me a call! It's time for a coaching session!

Seriously, if your work is not interesting to you, it will be hard to make it sound interesting to anyone else either. Maybe what you need is to take a break from work for a while – even a week, if that's all you can manage – to come back with fresh eyes. (Take a look at your interests from Unit 2, and choose one interest to guide you for the week's itinerary.) On the other hand, maybe you need to re-engage with your profession. Join an industry group. Attend a well-placed conference. Serve on a panel of speakers. Take or teach a class. Find a way to reinvigorate your passion, so that you can convey that passion to others. As you are doing these things, observe the interactions that energize you and the reactions of those who seem to really "get" who you are and what you do. Don't forget to take notes!

D. THE PAPER PLATE CHALLENGE

I mentioned at the outset of this chapter that getting your own name right in your elevator pitch is not the challenge. So here is the challenge, or rather, here is my challenge for you. I call this the "paper plate challenge" because, well, it is a challenge and it involves a paper plate. Please get one now. In fact, get a whole stack of them. Then get a Sharpie® or another permanent marker, or, if you are a fan of colors, get two or three.

Yep, you guessed it. You are going to write out your elevator pitch on that plate. If you are environmentally conscious, you might consider writing on the back of the plate, so you can still eat off the front. If you are highly social, you might invite a few close friends, pour a glass of something bubbly, and make it a plate party. Either way, if your message doesn't fit on the plate, it is too long to be an elevator pitch.

Here are six things we consistently get wrong when formulating and delivering elevator pitches:

1) We don't base them off of our personal value propositions but instead try to pull them out of the air (hence the three-part pyramid in Unit 1).

2) We can't stop talking about ourselves (hence the "plate" limit).

3)   We don't phrase our pitches in terms of benefits for the person with whom we are speaking (review the benefits you enumerate in Unit 7).

4)   We try to create a single, bulletproof elevator pitch for all possible situations, while we should be creating a responsive set of points that we can mix and match for our various audiences (hence the multiple plates at the ready).

5)   We don't sound excited when we deliver our elevator pitches (and we wonder why no one else is either).

6)   We have a presentation problem, such as speaking too softly, not pausing to catch a breath (or let anyone ask a question), getting off topic or engaging in some other form of self-sabotage in our delivery (which is corrected by practice, feedback and a strong message that we can confidently project).

Which of the above, if any, is my stumbling block:

_____

_____

How I can fix that:

_____

_____

_____

I include "equivalents" on the following pages, although I can assure you (having done this with groups) that actual plates are much more fun and make this challenge feel less formal and intimidating. After all, what could be easier than writing with a permanent market on a disposable plate? If you don't like what you wrote, you can always write another one.

If you want immediate feedback on your ideas, hold a "paper plate" night with colleagues and other professionals who want to create their own elevator pitches, with or without the bubbly drink that I mentioned above. Each of you can write on one or more plates and then present aloud to each other what you have written. Ask what was most compelling about your pitch. Then ask your audience to repeat what you said, and see how it matches what you actually presented. (You may be surprised what they actually heard and what they missed!) See if you can keep your pitch to two minutes (or less). If you don't, laugh it off, make notes to improve and try it again.

Remember – don't reinvent the wheel! Turn back to page 117 if needed.

Elevator Pitch Challenge

(here's backup if you don't have a plate handy,
or you can transfer your answers here):

Target audience:

Elevator Pitch: Variation 1

Target audience:

Target audience:

CONCLUSION

A final congratulations on completing all of the units in this book!

Now that you have invested your efforts to create your value proposition, don't just shelve and forget it. Create a plan for yourself to review your value proposition periodically (once every quarter, six months or year). One way to keep on track is to go right now – yes, now! – to your calendar and set up the dates for your next two to four reviews.

As part of your review, you may wish to do some or all of the following:

- Reread some or all units of this workbook

- Complete any sections that you may have left blank or wish to revise

- Ponder one key question (of your choosing) and make a corresponding change in your professional life

- Create additional action items (see page 18)

- Record another two-week tracker on meaning or flow (or another area of priority)

- Compare your value proposition, branding and/or elevator pitch to how your career has evolved

- Challenge yourself to learn a new skill or create the environment to grow a talent

Significant changes I expect (or hope) for my career in the coming **six months**:

Significant changes I expect (or hope) for my career in the coming **12 months**:

My commitment to leveraging what I have already done here (with 10 as the highest):

1   2   3   4   5   6   7   8   9   10

My plan for upcoming periodic reviews (content and schedule of dates and times):

What I would like to achieve in my next periodic review:

What I would like to achieve in subsequent reviews:

How I can keep myself on track:

FINAL NOTES

If you have other notes you would like to include in this workbook, and they do not fit in the pages above, please use the space below or tuck in additional pages. Remember, writing clarifies and cements concepts and prepares you for the big sprint – or marathon!

_____

_____

_____

_____

_____

_____

_____

_____

_____

_____

_____

_____

_____

_____

ABOUT THE AUTHOR

ANNE MARIE SEGAL is a career and leadership coach, resume strategist, author and speaker who works with attorneys, executives and entrepreneurs.

Anne Marie has worked with hundreds of professionals on career transitions, advancement, leadership, job interview preparation, resume writing and personal branding. With 15 years of experience as a corporate attorney prior to coaching (including 10 years focused on hedge funds and private equity), coupled with earlier study and work in the arts, Anne Marie is a grounded, practical and industry-savvy coach and writer. She relishes helping professionals unlock advancement in their careers by recognizing, enhancing and communicating their value.

Anne Marie holds a J.D. from New York University School of Law, an M.A. in Art History from The University of Chicago and a B.A. in Fine Arts (Photography) from Loyola University of Chicago. She received her coaching certification as a Certified Career Management Coach and is also a Certified Professional Resume Writer.

In October 2016, Anne Marie published *Master the Interview: A Guide for Working Professionals*, available online through Amazon, Barnes & Noble and a host of independent booksellers. *Know Yourself, Grow Your Career: The Personal Value Proposition Workbook* is her second book. She is a frequent public speaker and has been invited to present to the United Nations (ICTY/MICT), University of Chicago, Association of Corporate Counsel, United Way and National Resume Writers Association, among other organizations.

Anne Marie is available to discuss private, one-on-one leadership, career and business coaching and writing. Please reach out through the contact form on her website or email her at asegal@segalcoaching.com.

For questions about the book, please direct inquiries to knowyourself@segalcoaching.com.

Made in the USA
Middletown, DE
12 September 2017